The Practicing Photographer

Essays on Developing Your Photographic Practice

By Ben Long

CDP Press

La Grande, Oregon

completedigitalphotography.com

The Practicing Photographer
Copyright © 2021 Ben Long and CDP Press

ISBN 978-1-7326369-4-1 (print)
978-1-7326369-5-8 (ebook)

ALL RIGHTS RESERVED. No part of this work covered by the copyright herein may be reproduced, transmitted, stored, or used in any form or by any means graphic, electronic, or mechanical, including but not limited to photocopying, recording, scanning, digitizing, taping, Web distribution, information networks, or information storage and retrieval systems, except as permitted under Section 107 or 108 of the 1976 United States Copyright Act, without the prior written permission of the publisher.

Prismatic Spring (front cover) © Rick LePage;
Author photo (back cover) ©Keith Carter

Editor: Rick LePage

Published by CDP Press, LLC
P.O. Box 849, La Grande, Oregon 97850

completedigitalphotography.com
info@completedigitalphotography.com

For Fred, Byron and Gary,
who taught me
all the important stuff.

Contents

vii   Forward, by Keith Carter
ix   Introduction, by Rick LePage

Practicing

3   Why practice?
5   Practice by any other name
7   Practice takes practice
9   Remove the obstacles to shooting
10   To Instagram or not to Instagram
11   Search out group critiques
13   Practicing photography is hard

Before Shooting

17   Artistry is learned
18   Study the past
20   How to look at photos
22   Train your eye through photo books
23   Photographers for your consideration
25   Exposure isn't everything
27   Understanding your medium
29   Learn what seeing feels like

Shooting

33   Look for interesting things
35   It takes work to find a photograph
37   The difference between "of" and "about"
39   What does "comfort zone" really mean?
41   Shoot first, ask questions later
42   Fill your media card
44   Get into a rut
45   Making choices
47   Work with your eyes, not your brain
48   Always be a photographer

50 "Pretty" photos matter
52 Shoot sketches

Mind Games

57 Am I good?
58 Why do other people's photos look better than mine?
60 Fear
62 Clichés
64 Maybe it's not a cliché
65 Don't control the shoot before you start
66 "What if I'm stupid?"
68 Things going wrong can be good news
69 Take the "why not" shot
70 Passion and boredom

Post-Production

75 Less is more
77 Editing vs. editing
80 Good Photoshop is not good photography
82 The most powerful tool in your image editor
83 In praise of the small print
85 Another use for printing

Presentation

89 Build your portfolio
91 Tips for building a portfolio
93 A strong body of work takes time
95 Maybe you don't know enough yet
96 Wrestling with the artist's statement
98 Titles
99 What does a sale mean?
101 Getting your project out into the world

Coda

105 Developing a practice strategy
111 Is my practice successful?
114 Other Resources

Forward

Ben Long is a wonderful teacher. He is both experienced and understanding of the underpinnings of what it takes to create both an enduring artist, and a coherent body of work. The subjects he writes about here are not exactly sexy, but they are critical to building your own photographic practice, and developing an enduring body of work, or even a career.

Why make photographs? What can you expect from them? Why put yourself through the paces, the expenditures of money on materials, large blocks of time spent pursuing ideas you might not be able to finish, and the modest anguish with dumb-ass philistines who just don't get it? Why look at art? People make art for many reasons, chief among them the fact there are things human beings feel the need to express that are beyond language. The lessons gleaned from *The Practicing Photographer* are essential for both photographers and viewers who want to try to answer these questions.

Robert Frost once said finding your own voice was like *"having a lover's quarrel with the world."* Making photographs is more or less a solitary occupation. Subject matter comes from what you are disposed to think about, what issues concern you, what you believe is worth exploring, and how courageous you are with spending your precious time. Murmur a few hopeful words, wield the camera like a magic wand, and on a good day, you can conjure up proof of a dream.

I believe that Ben's book is a much-needed guide to navigating technique, aesthetics, decision-making, development of an ideal portfolio, exhibition preparation, writing an artist statement, and much, much, more. You've heard the cliché: "I don't know anything about art, but I know what I like," but people are often wrong on both counts. They know too much that is wrong about art; and they don't know what they like—they know what they are supposed to like.

We've come a long way, both aesthetically and technically, from the dazzling days when thirty-four-year-old one-time junior bank clerk, George Eastman from Rochester, New York, introduced a simple box camera loaded with film and "You push the button and we do the rest." If you would like to elevate your work, and broaden your current thinking of what constitutes meaningful work, *The Practicing Photographer* is the ideal book to keep close at hand.

Keith Carter

Introduction

I've known Ben for nearly 30 years, and, for almost all of that time, he and I have been like long-lost twin brothers, obsessed with photography (and motorcycles). We spent many days in the 1990s discussing the nascent world of digital photography: early Photoshop; cool medium-format film cameras and crappy low-res digital cameras; low- and high-end film scanners, and more. I can still remember his phone call in October 2000, where he could barely hide his glee over photos from Canon's first real digital SLR, the D30 — which I ordered immediately after our call.

Over the years of our friendship, Ben has, to echo Keith Carter's words, become a consummate teacher of all things photographic. Sure, he knows gear and lighting and composition and camera settings, and he has written one of the defining tomes on photography in the 21st century, *Complete Digital Photography*, but Ben is truly at his best when he talks about practice. You can see this in the popularity of Ben's weekly video series on LinkedIn Learning, "The Practicing Photographer." And, when I teach these concepts in workshops, many students find resonance in Ben's concept of building your own photography practice.

This book grew out of many discussions over the years about practicing; how to do it, how to maintain it, and how to use it to grow as a photographer. Our goal was to produce a short book of essays that one could read in bits and pieces, almost as a "Way to Photography." We didn't want a rehash of the LinkedIn series — although there are some essays here that were inspired by ones in the series — we wanted a guidebook for people who were looking for an alternative path to becoming a better photographer that didn't involve buying new gear. Yes, gear is important, but mastering the gear component alone won't necessarily make you better.

When planning *The Practicing Photographer*, we made the decision not to use a single photograph inside its covers. As you will discover in the pages to come, viewing photographs, especially ones by great photographers past and present, is a significant element of Ben's practice regimen. This book, however, is intended to be a map more than a monograph, and we didn't want to clutter it with superfluous photographs.

We hope you enjoy it, but more importantly, we hope it helps you on your photographic journey.

Rick LePage
Publisher, CDP Press

PRACTICING

In the late 1970s, a family friend named George Shaw wrote a doctoral dissertation on how one teaches and learns jazz improvisation. To research this project, he was given a grant to travel about the country interviewing musicians about how they learned. He made audio recordings of these interviews — more than 200 of them — and they form an amazing document about how an entire generation of musicians learned their craft.

In every interview George asks the subject how they practiced. My favorite answer to this comes from the blues legend Muddy Waters:

GEORGE: *Did you ever practice?*

MUDDY WATERS: *Yeah.*

GEORGE: *What'd you practice?*

MUDDY WATERS: *The blues.*

While most of the subjects had more elaborate answers, what I find especially interesting is that George chose to ask this question. Not because he wondered if practice was necessary, but because he knew that practice is a skill in itself and that there are as many approaches to practice as there are musicians.

The same is absolutely true for photography. As with any other discipline that requires practice, some methods and approaches will work better for some people than others. In this section we're going to take a look at issues surrounding the idea of practice with the goal of helping you improve your own photo practice regimen.

Practice is something that you need to actively think about. In fact, practice is something you have to practice. It might take some experimentation and a few tries before you find the practice system that works best for you, and that system will change over time. Hopefully these essays will help you find the beginnings of your own, meaningful practice.

Why practice?

Your goal as a photographer should not be to take great photos.

Don't get me wrong, your goal as a photographer should not be to take lousy photos either, but building your goals around the idea of a final product often keeps you from engaging in the processes that make you a better photographer.

Studying theories of composition, guidelines for exposure, and best practices for shooting are all important. I certainly spend plenty of time teaching those things, and you do need to invest time in learning them. But such study will only take you so far. What will make you a better photographer is figuring out how to improve your photographic self. Some of the ways you might achieve this include:

- Learning how to consistently see the world photographically.
- Learning how to defeat the editors and other negative thought processes that you carry around in your head.
- Discovering the unique characteristics of your way of seeing the world, so that you're expressing your own ideas rather than simply copying someone else's.
- Learning to combat boredom.
- Adapting to changes in your own interests and tastes, over time, and learning how those changes affect your photography.
- Striving to understand what makes a successful photograph work.

None of these practices follow any rules or theories. They are not things you can learn by rote, but they are necessary if you want to move beyond the simple, process-oriented, "eight ways to improve your photos" type of instruction that you find littered around the web.

The key to all of this is practice. Unfortunately, most of us learn our ideas about practice at a young age, when we're learning either a sport or a musical instrument. In my middle-school orchestra class we had "practice report cards." Each week, we were required to log at least 30 minutes of practice every day, and then have our parents notarize this document, which was critical to our final grade. While this did get me to saw away on the cello for a lot of hours, it also taught me that practice is a particular activity that you engage in, and that it's different and separate from performance or playing for pleasure.

Years later, I found myself working for a number of jazz musicians. From them, I saw a very different attitude and approach to practice. The first thing you notice about the practice habits of professional musicians is quantity: they practice a lot. But what also struck me was how much they thought about their process of practicing. They discussed it with each other, they experimented with it, trying different approaches and different disciplines. Practice, it turns out, is something you have to practice. This is why I don't buy the "10,000 hours to achieve mastery" idea. Number of hours isn't as important as quality of hours, and figuring out how to get quality hours takes some work.

But for all of these people, practice was not seen as an activity that was necessarily separate from the other playing that they did — rather, there was only playing. I asked one musician friend, on the night before his wedding, what he was going to do the following morning, since the wedding was not until the afternoon. "I think I'll practice," he said. "It relaxes me."

As a kid, I had never considered the idea of practice as something enjoyable, let alone relaxing, but if you practice enough it becomes a comfortable, familiar activity — a relaxing place to go where you can engage with your own strengths and lose yourself in something familiar.

Practice is a state of mind that you should, ideally, be living in as much as possible. Every time you pick up your camera, you're practicing; every time you look through a book of photographs you're practicing; every time a play of light catches your eye and causes you to think about it, you're practicing. If you make practicing your goal then you'll be reshaping yourself into someone with a stronger visual sense, who has an easier time achieving a state of mindful interaction with the world, who is possibly more relaxed, likely more curious, and who lacks the achievement-oriented mindset that makes for self-defeating thoughts. And, as a nice benefit, all of this will lead you to take better photos.

Practice by any other name

One of the biggest obstacles to learning is language. We don't all hear the same words and phrases with the same meaning. If you're stuck on a particular problem, you can often get unstuck by trying to change the language that describes that problem.

Many people have trouble with the concept that seeing and photography are things that you can practice, because of the particular meaning that they assign to the word practice. So before we get too far into the depths of this idea of practice, I want to offer a simple language hack that you can employ that might make all of this easier to understand. I learned this hack from a friend.

Regina Saisi has been a theatrical improviser for over 40 years. She makes up full-length stories, on a stage, in real-time. She also practices a lot. "Improv" and "practice" seem to be antithetical concepts, but of course there is a methodology to improvisation. I brought this up one day, and her reply was very interesting: "Oh, I don't think of it as practice," she said, "I think of it as *working out*."

People often perceive practice as a process of running drills of a predefined type—you practice a piece of music over and over, you execute a particular sports play over and over. That's the model of practice that most of us know. But when your medium requires you to find or generate content on the fly—something that most types of photography require—then there's nothing to actually drill when you're practicing.

Since Regina has nothing to drill she instead thinks about developing—or working out—specific improv muscles. She and her fellow improvisers create exercises that develop a reflex to say yes to things; they engage in rapid-fire games designed to foster spontaneity; they repeatedly make up scenes that are specifically intended to exercise their understanding of status or character or narrative.

They do not practice particular scenes or moments or building blocks of scenes—everything presented on-stage truly is made up in-the-moment. Instead, they "work out" the thought processes, emotional reflexes, and self-awareness that allows them to do the work.

Many photographic exercises might take on a different feeling if you shift to thinking about working out. Learning to recognize compositional elements that span different planes in space is a perspective that you can work out, so is learning to recognize good black-and-white subject matter, good shallow depth-of-field subjects, the interplay of light and shadow, and on and on.

I use the word "practice" a lot. If you find yourself struggling with reconciling your idea of the word practice with what you know of the discipline of photography, then feel free to replace "practice" with "working out" or "exercising," or whatever word works for you. Practice takes practice, and you have to find the mechanisms that are effective.

Your practice process is unique to you; don't hesitate to alter or change any aspect of it, including the very words you use to describe it.

Practice takes practice

One of the first decisions to make when creating some kind of practice regimen or program is to have goals. George Shaw, while interviewing the New Orleans-based jazz clarinetist Alvin Batiste, asked him if he practiced. Batiste described the practice process he used when he was starting out, when he also had a full-time job.

"When I came home from work I'd get an alarm clock," explained Batiste, "and set it for eight hours to ensure that every day I got in the eight hours of practice that I wanted."

"That was after work?" asked George.

"Yeah, after work."

"So what did you practice?"

"Whatever I wasn't good at."

"You mean certain tunes?"

"Tunes or parts of tunes."

A practice regimen can be as simple as that: eight hours a day on things you're not good at. Not that I would describe eight hours of practice after an eight-hour workday as "simple," but my point still stands.

George once told me of his own practice plan. He knew that he wanted to get in a certain number of hours of practice a day, so he would set a timer for that length, and then start practicing. But of course, he also had other things going on in his life. He was a college administrator and a working musician, so invariably things would interrupt him. When the phone rang, or an appointment came up, or if he got bored, then he would stop the timer and not start it up again until he returned to his practice. If he had quit because he was bored, he would not go back until he had regained his interest. He said that might take a couple of hours, but that it always came back and, at the end of the day, it didn't matter that his practice was not contiguous because practicing when you're uninterested doesn't yield any benefit.

As a photographer you can choose to define a time goal, or an image-count goal. Maybe you want to shoot 100 images a day, or produce two finished images a day, or in a certain amount of time. If that goal is terrifying or intimidating then set a different one: shoot fifteen images a day, or actively engage in shooting for half an hour. The specific plan doesn't matter — what does matter is to have a goal. That goal will change over time with interest, other events in your life, and your skill level.

You want your practice to be engaging. If you've zoned out and are simply going through the motions, then you'll be better served by setting the practice aside for a bit, and trying to get re-energized. But again, as long as you have some kind of metric that you're trying to achieve, then it won't matter if you're coming and going to the practice. By the end of the day, you'll get it all done.

As for what a photographer should practice, that could be anything from the technical to the creative. What's more, sometimes practicing one will inform the other. For example, you might spend a week saying "Today I'm going to shoot images with very shallow depth of field." That will definitely engage you in what is probably a very different way of seeing, especially if you really embrace the exercise and aim for images with a lot of smeary blur. But the process of achieving those shots will also work your technical understanding of depth of field.

Alternatively, you might choose to spend some time each day looking through photo books, training your eye by studying the work of great photographers, past and present. (I'll talk more about why this is so important in the next section of the book.)

If you have trouble finding time to practice, then look to work it into another part of your day. Maybe you need to walk your dog, or you walk to get exercise. Perhaps you find that you can do that chore first thing in the morning, before you go to work, and build a photo project around it. Aim to get one good image from that walk every single day.

Again, practice takes practice. You need to find the mechanisms that motivate you, that you'll follow through with, and that will shore up the parts of your skill and talent that you think need help. For most of us, that will be far less practice than Alvin Batiste's eight hours. For you, it might not be every day. You'll have to do some thinking to figure out that process, and you'll definitely need to adjust your regimen as you continue with it, but the process begins with the simple questions of "what to practice?" and "how long?"

Remove the obstacles to shooting

Because you enjoy something, it's easy to think that you will always want to do it, but that's not necessarily true. I have said that your goal as a photographer should be to practice, but the fact is that practice is work. Photography requires thought and, sometimes, emotion; it almost always requires getting out of your chair and going somewhere. And with all of that comes risk — the risk of coming back unsatisfied with what you've shot. And so you find ways to avoid practice. Surprisingly, some of the ways that you avoid practice might not be especially sophisticated, which is what makes them easy to overcome.

Here's how far the drive not to practice can go for me. I have a number of cameras, which live on shelves in my apartment. I rarely use any kind of dedicated camera bag. Instead, I put my camera and lenses into a backpack or motorcycle bag or whatever else I happen to be taking with me. That means that going out to shoot requires some extra effort: I have to round up gear and get it into a bag. I know that hardly counts as "effort" but it's still enough of a hassle that it can keep me from going out to practice. So now I always keep one street-ready kit packed up at all times, so that I don't have the extra excuse of preparation getting in the way of me doing what I need to do.

Maybe you're not as lazy as I am, or maybe you always have a camera in a bag, but I would recommend that if you want to make yourself practice more with your camera, or even to make yourself shoot more, figure out what physical obstacles are in the way of you and the process of shooting. Does your camera need to be in a bag so you can quickly head out to shoot? Does it need to be out of a bag so that you are more likely to grab it? Maybe for you the obstacle isn't access to your camera. Pay attention to your own habits and see if there's something that you use as an excuse to allow yourself to not do your work. Obviously, there can be mental obstacles that get in the way as well, and we'll talk about some of those later. They tend to be harder to fix so, for now, get the easy physical obstacles out of your way.

To Instagram or not to Instagram

Photography serves many purposes. To a photographer it can be a form of expression, a source of income, or both, but we also use photography to document things: daily life, vacations, parties, family photos, and more. And, with social media outlets, photography has become a medium of everyday communication more than ever before.

When most people post a photo to social media, they post using a particular photographic voice. If you're trying to practice a different voice, and want to focus on that, then continually returning to the safe confines of your social media voice might be hamstringing your practice goals. Then again, it might not. As I said, the important thing is to ask this question.

I recently had a discussion with Marwin Begaye, a friend who is a professor of printmaking at a university, and an accomplished printmaker. I asked him if he thought he could see a difference in his students' output since the rise of Instagram. I figured that he might need a moment to ponder his answer, but he didn't. He immediately replied:

"Yes, there are four things: people no longer consider light and shadow in their prints; they create prints of single objects rather than objects that are within a context of other things, or set on a background; they create very literal, realistic images rather than images with some style or interpretation; and they no longer work big — everything is five to seven inches wide."

In his mind, these trends started with the rise of Instagram and, in fact, his list does a pretty good job of describing an Instagram photo.

It doesn't really matter whether you think any of those are limitations or negatives, the point is that he can see a change in the visual sense of his students since they started spending so much time looking at and creating social media images. Instagram photos are often driven by trends and styles and fads. It's easy to be taken in by those, and they can be very limiting. As a visual artist, if you want to ensure the integrity of your practice, and you want to work in an environment that's free of influence and compromise and distraction, then you should look very closely at how your social media photography impacts the more serious work that you do. Maybe it does, maybe it doesn't; what's important is that you *know*.

Search out group critiques

A group critique is a common part of photo classes and workshops, and a regular feature at art schools. An assignment is given, and the participants submit a predefined number of images for that assignment. Then, together, the group critiques and discusses the images. Depending on the instructor, you might have different levels of group engagement, but the point is that there are many voices involved. This process terrifies a lot of people, but here are three reasons why group critiques will make you a better photographer.

Group critiques give you a vocabulary for assessing and discussing photographs. When you look at one of your own images or someone else's images, you will have to find words to describe your feelings about the image. Together, as a group, you might build on each other's words until you have a refined vocabulary for discussing why a particular image works, or why it doesn't work. You will then recycle that vocabulary and improve on it. As you engage in more critique sessions you will find that when you have a feeling about something you can more quickly get to an articulation of that feeling.

While all of that will help you in future critique efforts, the more significant value is that, when you're out in the field with a camera to your eye, and you feel like there's something off about your composition, you'll have the vocabulary to describe it to yourself. That will make it easier to identify the problem, which will make you more likely to find a solution. This is the real power of critique: it teaches a vocabulary that will change the way that you shoot.

No one sees the world in the same way. Everybody has a unique vision. Does that mean that everybody's vision yields great photographs? No. But everyone sees the world in their own way, which means that they all interpret images in slightly different ways. Sometimes, it's quite interesting to see what other people see in your work, things that you hadn't seen yourself.

Sometimes the way that you see the world can work against you. Since you see the world in your particular way, it can become boring to you, and lead you to second-guess yourself into believing that a shot is better than it is. Group critiques will remind you that what looks obvious to you might not look obvious to other people. The flip side of that, of course, is that an image that you think looks fantastic might elicit little more than a "yeah, that's nice" from the group. While that reaction might be disappointing, it's also instructive.

A group critique will make your photos less precious. That may not sound like a desirable thing, but feeling precious about your images is not a great place to be, insofar as your creative process is concerned.

It's possible for you to get too close to an image, to get obsessed with every detail and get finicky about your edits. I'm talking about those times when you absolutely can't decide if the version that's slightly more yellow in the sky is better than the one that's a tiny bit more neutral in the sky. I've gotten lost in those kinds of obsessions and shown the versions to people and gotten "Doesn't matter, they're both fine." Group critiques can help you strip some of that finickiness off your post-production process. Losing that will also help if you're one of those people who has trouble trying to choose a small number of selects out of a larger batch.

If the idea of a group critique makes you uncomfortable, try to remember that everyone else in the room is in the same boat. When your images come up, it's very easy to feel like you're in the spotlight, but you're not. As far as the audience is concerned they're just looking at more images in a long series of images.

Think about your own response to looking at other people's images. Do you pass judgment on them? Do you make assumptions about them? Do you project things on to them? Most likely you don't, so it's safe to assume that no one else is doing that to your images, either. Everyone else wants what you want: to improve their skill level.

In a conservatory or art school environment, critiques can be brutal. But in a typical camera club environment, workshop, or community college class environment, it's not that rough. You should be able to find a critique environment that suits your temperament. Your first one is going to be the worst, but it will get easier from there.

> If you have access to LinkedIn Learning, there is a two-part Practicing Photographer called "How To Critique A Photo." In it, you'll see me critique images submitted by LinkedIn employees while discussing things you might look for and think about when critiquing someone else's images. (cdp.pub/critique)

Practicing photography is hard

A good photo is the confluence of many things: an interesting subject in good light, a photographer who happens to have a camera ready at that moment, along with the requisite skill level to get the shot. Given how many factors have to converge in the right way, it's amazing sometimes that great, candid photos exist at all.

Every time you carry a camera it is with the hope that events will conspire to give you a great photographic opportunity. This means that, as a photographer, you're always "on the job" when you have a camera with you. Some part of you is always hoping and scoping for a great shot. There's nothing wrong with keeping your eyes open for great opportunity; having drive is important, and the satisfaction of being surprised by a great opportunity is wonderful. But if you're always on the job, when do you practice?

Perhaps a more important question to ask is, "When do you let yourself practice?"

You can say, "I'm going to go practice," but if some part of you is holding out hope for that great shot, then you're possibly going to be disappointed when you come home, even if your intent was only practice. More importantly, you may not be staying in the frame of mind that is necessary for an effective practice session.

For example, say you're given the simple exercise of "go explore slow shutter speed." So you head out with the idea of practicing and experimenting with blurring motion and introducing intentional camera shake and smear. Those are technical skills that require practice; learning to pan and follow a moving subject is hard. To benefit from that practice you need to focus on the manual dexterity required to get the shot. You don't need to be thinking about producing a great final image.

If you're still holding out hope that you're going get a great, keeper shot, then you may not allow yourself to be in the loose, relaxed state necessary to practice the single skill that we're talking about. What's more, coming back disappointed because you didn't get a great shot will make it harder to be motivated to practice in the future.

The easiest way to effectively practice is to define your measure of success before you go out. State specifically that your goal is to practice and, more specifically, to practice a specific thing. When you come home and review your images, if it turns out that you did practice your specific goal, then you have succeeded, regardless of the quality of your images.

It's easy to come up with your own practice routines based on the types of things you like to shoot, or basic exercises like limiting yourself to a specific shutter speed, aperture or focal length. If you're looking for more ideas, there is a list of practice suggestions in "Developing a practice strategy" on page 105. You can also download my free supplemental exercise PDF, which is a companion workbook to *Complete Digital Photography, 9th Edition* (**cdp.pub/exercisebook**). Not all of these will be right for everyone, but I encourage you to try them.

BEFORE SHOOTING

The photographer Joe Buissink once said that when he's out walking around without a camera, he will snap his fingers every time he sees a potential photo. In this way he manages to exercise some of his photographic sense even when he doesn't have a camera with him. Obviously, that's a great exercise for any photographer, but it also shows that there's much you can do to improve your photography, even when you're not shooting or processing images.

In this section we're going to look at some activities and practices you can engage in, and some ideas you can mull, when you're not shooting. These are things that you can do before you go shooting, or when you're between shoots. In these essays, we're going to explore the nature of seeing, look at a few different ways to improve your ability to see, and detail one of the most significant practices you can undertake to improve your photography.

While you might sometimes find yourself lacking the time or opportunity to engage in as much photography as you'd like, that doesn't mean you have to take a break from your photography practice. There are plenty of valuable ways to shore up your skill set, even when you don't have a camera in your hands.

Artistry is learned

There is nothing special required to be an artist. Artists are not different, a breed apart, or possessed of any special level of creativity. The fact is, everyone is creative, whether it's in their daily lives or their profession. "Creative" accountants, for example, have probably had more impact on the world in the last fifteen years than anyone we usually consider to be creative.

Artistic process is learned. Musicians learn to hear pitch and meter, painters learn to translate scale and proportion into gesture, poets develop a relationship to vocabulary and grammar that allows them to transpose emotions into words. Yes, there are people who have a natural affinity for some of these things — or, in the case of perfect pitch, a reportedly genetic advantage — but that affinity simply means that they get a head start on the learning process. The "naturally gifted" person gets to skip the first few lessons that the rest of us have to take. But those people still require a tremendous amount of study and, as importantly, thousands of hours of practice, before they can achieve even limited mastery of their craft. A natural talent that gives someone a head start in the learning doesn't translate into the ability to ultimately create better, more advanced work than someone who struggled through their entire education.

Photographers have lots of mechanical skill and theory to learn, but that's the easy part of the craft. The hard part is learning to see. Learning to recognize the raw material of a good photograph: forms, colors and tones. Learning to effectively translate those raw materials from the broad, three-dimensional world down to a limited two-dimensional image. All of that process is procedural. When you develop some mastery of it you will be less aware of the procedural process that you're engaged in, but it will still be there. That's the point of practice, to get those procedures learned to such a degree that you don't even know you're following them.

I say all this because, if you want to make progress pursuing an art or craft, then you must accept that artistry is a skill. It can be learned and, through practice, mastered. There is no litmus test that says that some people will be better at it than others. There is no inherent advantage that you must have. We all solve problems every day, and don't always know that we're solving them. Creative process is just a long chain of problems to solve. So set aside any concerns you may have of whether you're creative, artistic, or gifted. If you've got the will to work hard, you've got what you need.

Study the past

If I walk into a beginning photography workshop or class and ask the students who their favorite photographers are, I mostly get blank looks. Yet I know if I were to walk into a beginning writing class and ask students who their favorite writers are, I would get lots of responses.

It's hard to imagine trying to compose a piece of music if you've never listened to music, or writing a novel if you've never read a book. But for some reason, beginning photographers are not immediately struck by the notion that they should know something about the photographs that have come before them. Unfortunately, this seems to be the area of study that most photographers ignore.

Here are just a few of the reasons that a study of photo history is critical to your improvement as a photographer:

- Looking at other photos is a form of eye training. The more you look at other images the more your eye will get a sense of many different compositional ideas, as well as how to read a photograph. Eye training is a way to push your photographic skills toward a more intuitive space.

- Over the last nearly 200 years, a lot of photographers have solved a lot of problems. Technical problems, creative problems, aesthetic problems. There's no reason for you to re-invent those solutions. You can learn from what they did, and move forward to places they never got to. Photo history is not just something that happened a long time ago, it's a platform that you can stand on to reach higher.

- While originality is not a necessary criteria for a successful image, if you want to be original then you need to know what's come before.

- Looking at other people's photos can be tremendously inspiring. Whether it's a specific inspiration — an idea that's sparked by something that someone else has done — or the simpler inspiration of getting excited by good work and wanting to go try to create some on your own, working through a nice book of photos can recharge your batteries and get you motivated.

No one creates in a vacuum; creative process requires input, and some of the most valuable input comes in the form of the work that has preceded you. Learning what came before helps you develop a vocabulary for considering and discussing photographic ideas, whether you're discussing them with someone else or muttering to yourself while you shoot.

Finally, considering the work of the past matters because you should be curious about the world around you. If you're not, I'm afraid you're not going to fare very well in any creative, expressive endeavor.

How to look at photos

As photographers, we all struggle with the fact that looking at something doesn't necessarily mean you're seeing what's there. That's really the big obstacle to shooting good photos. But it's also true when you're looking at finished work. You can't assume that just because you're looking at a photo, you're getting what it has to offer. Like the rest of photography, looking at photos requires practice.

I believe that looking at other people's work is an essential part of your photographic practice, but when I say "look at a photo" I am not talking about social media. What I mean is that you should look at photo books or prints in a gallery. When you look at a photo book, or exhibit, you're looking at work that has been curated. That means that the photographer, or someone else, has chosen the photos because they possess a certain level of quality. You might come across very nice images in a social media feed, but is every single one deemed amongst the best by that photographer? Probably not. With a book or exhibit, you know you're getting images that have been chosen for particular aesthetic reasons. This doesn't mean that they are all great, or that you must like them, but they have at least a sense of importance as art.

With a book you're also seeing a unified body of work. Maybe it's all work related to a single project, or maybe it's related to a stage in a photographer's life, but most of the time the images that have been gathered have been grouped for a reason. It may be more of a thematic reason than a narrative reason, but there's still purpose behind the grouping of images. Learning to organize, sequence and present images is a skill in itself, so you need to look at examples of that process.

As with all forms of practice, if your goal when you look at a photo book is to learn, then you need to give some thought to how you do it.

First, take a pass through the work and simply look at the photos like a non-photographer would. Proceed through the images and partake of them, have your emotional response to them, and experience the work. You might even want to do that several times, or set the book aside after you've gone through it, to digest what you've seen. Looking at images to partake of them is different from looking at images to learn from them, and you don't want the learning to get in the way of a "regular" experience of the images.

When you're ready to look at the images critically, return to the work, start at the beginning, and move through each image, asking yourself questions. Why does the image work or not work? How does your eye move around the image and what makes it move that way? What attracts your attention, and when? Why did the photographer choose the point of view that they chose? Why did they choose color, rather than black and white?

You don't have to ask yourself all of these questions about each image. These are just suggestions, and your questions don't always have to be technical. For example, if you're looking at a book of portraits, consider the subject. What do you think they are thinking or feeling and what, in the image, is making you think that they're thinking or feeling that? How are they lit? What are they wearing? What else is visible in the frame and how does that impact your sense of the person?

Of course, in any photo there are plenty of technical topics to be considered. What focal length lens was used (you can guess by looking at the field of view, and sense of depth in the scene). Did the photographer choose to shoot with deep or shallow depth of field? Is the image perfectly exposed, or is there over- or underexposure? Where is the light source, what color is the light, and how was it modified?

Your technical questions don't all have to be about gear. Take a look at the entire scene and imagine what it was like to be there. That will often reveal obstacles that might not be obvious at first glance. You might find questions about how the photographer steadied the camera, how they got gear into that space, how they managed rapidly changing lighting conditions, and so on. As you identify these complications, think about how you might solve them. This is a way to get experience addressing difficult problems without having to face them yourself.

Asking these kinds of questions can make for very enjoyable puzzles, and they almost always increase your appreciation of the craftsmanship behind an image. While they might lessen the emotional connection to the image, in return you might gain a connection to the photographer, as you imagine what they had to go through to get the shot.

Train your eye through photo books

If we were in the same room and I were to start singing an ascending scale of *"do re mi,"* you would probably be able to sing the rest of the scale. This is because, over time, you've heard that scale enough that your ear has become trained to recognize it. Ear training is a standard part of music training for serious musicians; through repetition they learn to recognize pitch as well as specific intervals, chords and modes.

I believe that good photographers go through a similar form of eye training. The more you look at finished photos, the more you will recognize potential subject matter when in the field and, more importantly, the easier it will be to arrange the contents of your frame. Through eye training, you will move from a procedural composition process while you're shooting to a more intuitive composition process.

There's not really any particular method to eye training, it's simply something that happens as you view more images. You won't necessarily feel anything happening, and the results may not be apparent until you've logged many months, but I heartily believe that spending time looking at images from other photographers is essential, simply because of the way that it trains your eye.

I have had the great pleasure of teaching alongside many great photographers and whether their specialty was portrait, documentary, street shooting, abstraction, architecture or any other form, they all had one thing in common: to a person, they each have large libraries of photo books, which they regularly study.

The best example I can think of this is the photographer Kurt Markus. After a lengthy, very successful career photographing everyone from supermodels to A-list actors to former presidents, Kurt has largely retired from shooting. Yet, while staying at his house, I couldn't help but notice that the first thing he did after rising early in the morning was to go to his library and spend an hour looking at a book of photos. He's not actively shooting anymore, but he is still studying, still trying to figure it out, through practice and eye training.

Of all of the practice suggestions in this book, the simple process of looking at other images is probably the most effective, and easiest form of practice that you can engage in.

Photographers for your consideration

If you're ready to start looking at the work of some other photographers, you'll find yourself immediately facing the question, "Whose work should I look at?" As we approach the start of photography's third century, you're going to find a lot of well-known photographers. To help you get started, here's a list of photographers I believe are worth looking into.

I have a reason for including everyone on this list, but I'm not going to tell you any of those; finding your own reasons is part of the learning process. I should also say that I don't like the work of every photographer on this list. Looking at work you don't like is important: you might learn to like it, and thus expand your aesthetic, or you might figure out why you don't like it, and so improve your own skill set.

I've broken this list roughly into four timelines, from the beginnings of photography in the 1800s, through the 20th century, and up to today:

19TH CENTURY

Fredrick Scott Archer	Anna Atkins	Julia Margaret Cameron
Louis Daguerre	Alexander Gardner	Hill & Adamson
William Henry Jackson	Eadweard Muybridge	Nadar
Timothy O'Sullivan	William Fox Talbot	Carleton Watkins

EARLY 20TH CENTURY

Ansel Adams	Bernice Abbott	Eugene Atget
Anne Brigman	Imogen Cunningham	André Kertesz
Heinrich Kühn	Dorothea Lange	José Ortiz-Eschagüe
Man Ray	Aaron Siskind	W. Eugene Smith
Frederick Sommer	Edward Steichen	Alfred Stieglitz
Paul Strand	Edward Weston	August Sander

MID 20TH CENTURY

Diane Arbus	Richard Avedon	Brassai
René Burri	Harry Callahan	Robert Capa
Henri Cartier-Bresson	Gregory Crewdson	Daniel Coburn
Linda Connor	Mike Disfarmer	Robert Doisneau
William Eggleston	Elliott Erwitt	Walker Evans
Robert Frank	Ernst Haas	Robert Heineken

Before Shooting

Kenneth Josephson	Barbara Klemm	Josef Koudelka
Robert Lebeck	Saul Leiter	Danny Lyon
Gerard Malanga	Vivian Maier	Robert Mapplethorpe
Mary Ellen Mark	Ralph Eugene Meatyard	Joel Meyerowitz
Ray K. Metzker	Arno Rafael Minkkinen	Helmut Newton
Irving Penn	Bert Stern	Dennis Stock
William Wegman	Weegee	Garry Winogrand

LATE 20TH CENTURY — PRESENT

Nick Brandt	Edward Burtynsky	Paul Caponigro
Keith Carter	Binh Danh	Susan Derges
Susan Kae Grant	Emmet Gowin	Andreas Gursky
Pieter Hugo	Connie Imboden	JR
Priya Kambli	Mark Klett	Michael Lundgren
Sally Mann	Kurt Markus	Chris McCaw
Richard Misrach	Martin Parr	Paolo Pellegrin
Platon	Meghann Riepenhoff	Alison Rossiter
Sebastião Salgado	Pentti Sammallahti	Toshio Shibata
Cindy Sherman	Stephen Shore	Sandy Skoglund
Alec Soth	Hiroshi Sugimoto	Guy Tillim
Jerry Uelsmann	Carrie Mae Weems	Francesca Woodman

The above list, with links to available resources for these photographers, can be found online at cdp.pub/photographers.

The best way to experience photographic work is in a book, museum or gallery. If you don't have access to a bookstore with a good photo section, or if you don't want to spend your money on photo books, check your local library or university library. A nearby school with a good photo program will often have a decent selection of books as well. Used photo books and old auction catalogs (a surprisingly rich source of photos) can also be found inexpensively on sites like eBay, Powells, Allibris, and AbeBooks. See the *The Practicing Photographer* support page at cdp.pub/PPsupport for more resources for finding photo books.

Exposure isn't everything

I was recently poking around in a photography forum and found an interesting discussion about the composition of a particular image. It was a good discussion, and then someone chimed in with, "what were your exposure settings?" I hear this question in workshops and classrooms from time to time and I often wonder, "why are you asking that question?"

Don't get me wrong; if you're a beginner, there's a lot you can learn from knowing the exposure settings that were used for a given image. If you're still not comfortable with whether a big aperture creates a deeper or shallower depth of field, or if you still have trouble remembering which f-stop number corresponds to which aperture size, then yes, careful analysis and thought about the exposure settings in a photo that you're looking at can help you learn.

If you're a photographer who's already comfortable with your exposure theory, then you shouldn't be looking for a universal recipe for good photos. When someone asks about exposure settings, I worry that they're thinking "oh, I see a lot of images that I like that were shot with f/8, so I'll set my camera on f/8." That's not how good photography works.

Consider an image with shallow depth of field. Does it really matter if you know whether it was shot at f/1.8 rather than f/2.4? You might say that it does matter because you're thinking about spending extra money for an f/1.8 lens. But honestly, a better way to figure out the depth of field potential of a lens is to go to a camera store and try it out. Or rent the lens online and use it for a few days.

One of the most effective creative things we can do as photographers is choose to intentionally overexpose or underexpose things so as to plunge shadows into darkness, or to brighten highlights. When I look at exposure settings for a printed image, I don't actually know if there was intentional over- or underexposure because I don't know what the original metering was. Maybe in some situations I could figure it out. Maybe it's a scene shot in bright daylight, and I see that it was at ISO 100, and I know from the sunny 16 rule, that at ISO 100, f/16, at 1/100th of a second is a good baseline exposure. I could then work through the reciprocal calculations from there to figure out from the settings they have listed whether they over or under exposed. Maybe. That presumes that I'm right about my initial baseline assumption, and that the photographer didn't do any dodging and burning, in which case all bets are off.

If I'm a sport shooter, and I see an image of a race car going by, and the photographer has frozen the motion, I could look at shutter speed to get an idea of what kind of shutter speed they needed to freeze that particular motion. I could learn some things from that, but only if I'm being very, very thoughtful about translating what I'm seeing in those settings, into what I'm seeing in the image. Sometimes, you can effectively make that translation, sometimes you can't.

So, again, don't look at these settings with the idea that you're learning some simple set of parameters that will make you a better photographer. What makes you a better photographer is thoughtful practice, working your shots, experimenting, trying different things, constantly trying to look for a new image, and shooting a lot. As you're doing that, your exposure settings will be what you think are right at that given time. Those settings won't necessarily apply anywhere else.

Understanding your medium

Years ago I read an interesting travel memoir by Jeff Greenwald, called *Shopping for Buddhas*. In the book, Greenwald finds himself in Nepal and he wants to buy a statue of Buddha. Actually, he wants to buy the "best" statue of Buddha, and in the process of trying to find that best statue of Buddha, he comes to learn a lot about the art world in Nepal. For example, he learns who has the reputation for particularly good statues of Buddha and who doesn't, and so on.

As he explores more, he comes to realize that the only artworks that he sees in the region are devotional pieces — paintings and sculptures of various Himalayan deities. Coming from the Western world, he begins to wonder where the new, younger voices are. He looks for the "avant garde" — those artists who push the medium forward by breaking the old rules and trying new things. As he talks to more dealers and gets deeper into the Nepalese art world, he writes:

> "The most perfect art, according to the Nepalese, stems from the re-creation of perfected formulas. No attempt need be made to realign (much less to shatter) the age old symbolic infrastructure. Why? Because it isn't necessary....In Nepal, traditional art is believed to already contain the highest level of understanding possible....The sole responsibility of the artist is to express these formulas as faithfully as possible."

Greenwald's confusion was because he thought that the medium he was investigating was sculpture and that, as in the Western world, it was up to the artist to find subject matter and develop a skill and style and then express their chosen subject sculpturally. But he was wrong, the medium was not "sculpture" but rather "sculpture of Buddha."

As a photographer, it's important to understand your medium, and thinking that your medium is "photography" may not be leading you in the right direction. If you have a specialty, you need to give some thought to what the specifics of that specialty are. What are the aesthetics of, say, architectural photography? What are the things that you have to know as a portrait photographer that you don't, maybe, have to know about as a landscape photographer?

The word "photography" covers a lot of ground and you can't just say "I'm going to go study photography" and expect to end up with a skill set that's going to be what you need for a more refined, specialized form of photography. This all may sound like a simple observation, but I encounter a lot of students who don't realize that they need to study their specific part of the photographic world, and they need to study it intently to effectively develop and hone the aesthetic, vision, and skill set that they need to execute a specialized form of photography at the level that they'd like.

Learn what seeing feels like

Seeing requires practice.

Seeing photographically is a very active process — it's not something that just happens as you walk through the world. With practice, your ability to see photographically will grow. Perhaps the best evidence that seeing is an active, learnable process is the fact that you can improve as a photographer. Plainly, as you get better, some sort of change happens within your body.

When you're seeing well, it feels a particular way. You might describe it as "being in the zone" or "in a state of flow" or simply feeling that the world looks different than it does when you're not seeing as well. A photographer who's working well is very engaged with their sense of sight. You want to learn how to get to that type of engaged seeing as often as possible. There's a good chance that you've probably already experienced this type of seeing at some time in your life. If you can identify some of the times when you have seen with more engagement, and if you can remember what that felt like, then you'll have an easier time getting back to that state.

Trying to seek out memories of when you have been actively seeing is a valuable exercise. It's a way to learn what the experience of actively seeing feels like — to identify the destination that you want to get to when you're shooting. Seek out a quiet space, give yourself a little time, and try to think about instances as an adult when you've felt yourself seeing very actively. Some examples for me that I can think of:

- In a neighborhood that I'd lived in for ten years, I once took a walk to run some errands, rounded a corner and saw an enormous building in the distance that I'd never noticed before. This was not so much a case of being in the zone as being given a very strong demonstration of how easy it is to be out of the zone — to not see big, obvious things in your everyday environment.
- I was 25 or 26 when I first traveled to Europe. I remember very clearly how different my visual sense was when I was there. I noticed doorknobs, and staircase moldings, and sidewalk cut-aways and all sorts of everyday objects that I don't pay attention to at home. The reason, of course, was that all of these things were different from what I'm used to. Thinking about that experience gives me a pretty strong "sense memory" of what it was like to see the ordinary very clearly.

- This one's harder to explain. On three occasions over the last twenty years, I have been on public transportation and during the process of trying to get off of the train, I have looked at a stranger, usually about arm's length away, and seen them with great clarity and specificity. I didn't see them as another face on the subway, rather I saw the depth and texture of their bone structure and skin, I felt a full meaning of the expression on their face, I noticed a quality about their motion — they were intensely real and present for me. I believe that, for a moment, I saw the way a truly skilled portrait photographer sees. The experiences were so strong that, all these years later, I remember precisely where I was and what the person looked like. I have not learned to turn that feeling back on at will, but at least I know it exists and can strive to return to it.

Athletes know particular things about how their bodies work. They know where their strengths and weaknesses are, they know what physical traits they can exploit and which ones they need to work around or improve. The more you can know about your personal sense of seeing, the better you will be at figuring out how to improve it, trigger it, or make use of it. Pay attention to what seeing feels like, try to remember times when it has felt different. Learning the feeling of seeing will make it much easier to get better at regularly seeing photographically.

SHOOTING

A photographer friend once told me that one of the reasons that they like photography is that, for that 1/60th of a second when the shutter is open, they're in complete control of the world. They were making this comment largely in jest, but there's definitely something satisfying about placing the things around you into a sense of visual order, even if it's just for a fraction of a second.

While I've divided this book into sections, based on different stages of photographic process, it's important to understand that none of these stages stands alone. So while the essays in this section focus on shooting, every other essay in this book also has something to do with shooting. Photography is a multi-step, multi-disciplinary process, but each different step and discipline informs the others. You need to think about your shoot while you're planning, you need to think about post-production while you're shooting and you need to remember imagery and feelings from the shoot while you're working on edits in post-production.

So while this is the longest section of the book, shooting is not necessarily the most weighty part of the photographic process. With some images, the hard work might come before or after, and shooting is just a necessary chore along the way. With other images, what happens in the camera might be beyond any preconceived idea.

There is no single, defining part of the photographic process, there is only "photography."

Look for interesting things

I've lived in San Francisco for several decades, and as a photographer it's a strange place to be. On one hand, it's my familiar home town, so I rarely see photos here. On the other hand, it's a beautiful international photo destination. You can actually buy books of images with exact photo locations so that you can go take your own version of well-known (and much-photographed) spots.

There's nothing wrong with shooting expected, or common shots of a known location — such places are usually well-known because they deserve to be photographed. What's more, you might find your own personal spin on those locations, or see the site in a literally different light from what you're used to. And, of course, documenting your experiences is a big function of photography — not all shots are intended to be fine art.

I bring all this up because it demonstrates a problem that a lot of photographers can fall prey to in their normal shooting process: the mindset of going out to find photos. The best photographers never go in search of photos, for the simple fact that it is very, very difficult to recognize a photo with the naked eye. It's hard to visualize that particular crop that your camera takes. It's difficult to compress the three-dimensional world down to a flat two-dimensional image.

So no matter where you are, whether you're in a place that has very obvious photos, or a place that you might consider mundane, or somewhere that you're quite familiar with, you will have a hard time if you try to see finished images with your naked eye.

Instead, when you're out shooting, don't look for photos. Forget about the camera and look for things that are interesting to you. Go and look for things that capture your eye. Sometimes, that's going to be a subject like the Golden Gate Bridge — an obvious photo subject. In other cases, it might simply be a play of light or a play of shadow or a texture. This is where eye training comes into play. The more photos you've seen, the more you will see things that are interesting to your eye in a photographic sense.

It doesn't matter what it is that captures your eye or why you notice it — or even if it has the potential to be a good photo. All that matters is that you've seen something you find interesting. Once you have, then you can lift your camera and start trying to figure out if there's a photo there. The world and the things in it that interest you are your raw material.

Your camera is what you use to turn that raw material into a photo. The tricky part is learning to pay attention to what it is that interests you.

A lot of times you might think "hey, that's interesting," and then look closer and think, "but I can't imagine what the photo might be." Just because you can't imagine it, doesn't mean there isn't a photo there. A lot of times you can't tell what the photo is until you're looking through that viewfinder.

This approach will also help you develop your own style — and put your own visual stamp on the photographic world. What makes a great image is when the photographer has seen something interesting, and found a way to represent that as a photo. Follow what interests you, and let the photos come from that.

It takes work to find a photograph

I once found myself sitting in the courtyard of the Blue Mosque, in Istanbul. You've probably seen photos of the Blue Mosque: it's a spectacular building dating back to 1609. I was there on a lovely summer day, and had no agenda. People were milling about and it was an ideal place to find yourself with a camera. Yet I looked around and thought, "there's nothing to shoot here." As I had that thought, another part of my brain knew that it was ridiculous, but still I felt relieved, because if there was nothing to shoot, then I was off the hook. I could continue to just sit and observe.

But then my eye caught a play of light on a far wall — just a splash of light filtering down from the minarets and onto some hand-carved 17th-century stone. When I saw that I thought, "Okay I could take a picture of that."

I sat there for a bit longer, hoping the light would go away, but it didn't and finally I told myself, "You should shoot that because you're allegedly a photographer and all." I walked over and took the picture.

The result is not a picture worth talking about, but in taking it, something changed. I reminded myself that light is interesting. With that reminder I kept photographing and I started to see other things — a woman sitting on some steps, a little kid with a cellphone — and suddenly I was seeing again. Light was my entry back into having my eyes open, reminding me that photos can happen anywhere.

I was not stuck because of the place I was in, I was stuck because I wasn't doing the work of being a photographer.

With that in mind, I would like to challenge you with an exercise: go out and remind yourself that photography is work.

The good news is that you don't have to go to a faraway land to do that. Do it in your own backyard — go out and walk with your camera, and find some pictures. Or, if you don't have a backyard then go onto the street in front of your building.

You might think, "there aren't any pictures in my backyard." That's just a thought — one you can have anywhere (including a picturesque 17th-century mosque). I promise you, though, that there are pictures in your backyard.

You may have to hunt for these images, so for this exercise, let yourself off the hook. It doesn't matter if you come back with lousy pictures — you don't have to show these pictures to anybody. This exercise has two goals.

First, to remind yourself of the fact that seeing is an active process. It is something you have to go out and do. When I was sitting there at the Blue Mosque, I was waiting for the pictures to come to me. The reason I felt that there weren't any photos to be had was because there was not a parade of elephants walking by, or something else that was obviously a picture.

Second, this exercise will remind you of technical process. When I got up to shoot the light on the mosque wall I forced myself to start thinking about depth of field and apertures, and that got me to weighing less depth of field versus shooting in the sharpness sweet spot of my lens' aperture, and so on. Photography is a craft as much as an art, and craft is something that has to be practiced. So, if nothing else, heading out into the backyard to shoot some stuff is going to make you practice the craft aspect of photography.

This is a simple exercise, and it may not sound like much, but it's a good thing to do any time that you feel stuck, any time you feel complacent, or any time you're feeling smug.

Sometimes you have to be reminded that you have to make photos, not just take them. I did not find photos to take at the Blue Mosque because of the Blue Mosque. I found photos to take because I did the work of finding some. You can do that anywhere.

The difference between "of" and "about"

Elizabeth Greenberg is a wonderful photographer with a long tenure as an educator and administrator at Maine Media, a great educational facility in Rockport, Maine that offers everything from workshops to MFA programs. I had the chance to teach with her, and in the process heard her make a very interesting distinction between two different types of photos.

ELIZABETH GREENBERG: Spending many years teaching and looking at photographs and developing my own work, I've realized that, for me, pictures are either "of things" or "about things." In the best case, they're both. We can all make a picture of a house, a tree, a flower, a person. And if we're skillful in employing the technology in constructive ways, we make a nice photograph. But it might not have anything to say. Compare that to pictures that are about something. The difference is in how the photographer engages the medium of photography — how they used the tools that are inherent to the medium, thought about what's in the frame, what's not in the frame, their vantage point, their depth of field. How did they specifically interpret a subject and share that vision of it with a viewer of the photograph?

BEN LONG: So, a picture of something employs the technical craft skills that you have. It needs to be nicely composed and well-lit and properly exposed. It's that "about" thing that's really hard.

ELIZABETH: It is hard! It is very hard. And it takes practice. And so many students I work with sometimes think, "Okay, I have to have intent. I have to have ideas and go illustrate them, and go make pictures of my idea." And they still fall hollow, because they haven't actually interpreted their ideas. The "about" comes from the intuitive action of being creative, and being fluid with your tools, and really interpreting with your camera.

BEN: Okay, so I might have my grandfather's hat, and I take a photo of it. For me, the result is a photo about my grandfather. But there's nothing in the image that conveys that to anybody.

ELIZABETH: A viewer of that image might not be able to say "Of course, that's Ben's grandfather's hat." But, the way that you photograph it — is it light? Is it dark? How far away from the hat is the camera?

Is it right side up? Is it on the table? What's the context of the hat, and how are you showing it to us? Is it — as I might do — very fuzzy and blurry? Trying to make visible manifestations of what a memory might look like? Or is it sharp, intact, and crystal clear and within the viewer's ability to touch it? And then you think about the memories you have, and how you might photograph that hat to suggest those memories. Do all that and then take a photo of your grandfather's hat.

BEN: Do you feel that, when an image is about something, that the viewer can tell that even if they're not getting the same "about" that you intended?

ELIZABETH: Yeah, hopefully, they're not getting the same about. Hopefully, they're getting more than that. And I think that depends on how we make the picture, and direct the emotional response to it. Is it soft and dreamy? Is it hard and edgy? Is it contrasty and sharp and everything's in focus? How the photographer tells us what to think of that subject.

BEN: Directing them.

ELIZABETH: Yeah, directing them.

BEN: This is a great distinction, and something you have to think about when you're out in the field, but I think another really good exercise is to go back through your own photo archive and look at your images, and try to decide which ones are in the "of" category and which ones are in the "about" category. Have you achieved both? You can even keyword them that way.

ELIZABETH: And I would add that going back and looking through your work, when you identify certain things that are true to your vision, you start understanding what your artistic voice is. You connect the threads between the pictures. That doesn't mean that everything will always look like those, but you understand where you're coming from in making the work. And, you begin to shift from "I have a bunch of pictures" to "I have a body of work."

What does "comfort zone" really mean?

In any creative pursuit you'll often hear people extolling the virtues of "getting out of your comfort zone." What does that mean if you're a photographer? Should you carry a heavier camera? Take up war photography?

A student once asked me to look at their work because he said he wanted help with his compositions. His work was good, and in the places where I could find weaknesses in his compositions I would start to say "Here you might do this because..." and he would finish my sentence for me. He already knew every point that I was trying to make. I finally said "you already know this stuff, so what's the problem?" His answer was "I keep composing my photos in the same ways." The only thing I could think to say was "then don't do that anymore."

We broke for lunch and as I thought about the guy, I realized that I knew where he was at—what he was feeling. At some point, early on, those compositional things that he did over and over were new to him, and he liked them. He took great pride and sense of accomplishment in the work he was creating, and those feelings reinforced his tendency to compose using those ideas. But after so much time those ideas were no longer fresh; he felt like he was in a rut.

None of us want to come home at the end of a day of shooting and feel like we did a bad job. For this guy, shooting with these particular compositional "tricks" that he'd learned had ensured that he would come home feeling okay about himself as a photographer. He had established a comfort zone: a box of photographic ideas that he could work within, which would dramatically improve his chances of not feeling like a failure.

Unfortunately, your comfort zone eventually becomes uncomfortable. It becomes familiar and boring and you feel stagnant. The only way out, though, is to take a risk, the horrible risk of feeling like you're a lousy photographer.

After lunch I told him that, for the afternoon assignment, he was absolutely free to shoot all of those usual compositions that he naturally sees. I told him it was a good idea to continue practicing with those, because he might actually stumble into something new about them. In addition, however, I told him to try at least one new thing with every scene he was photographing. This approach allowed him a safety net; he could still go home with images that weren't terrible, but he would also be forced to start the practice of trying something different.

Leaving your comfort zone doesn't mean abandoning it. Instead, your goal should be to expand it. Continue to work within it, but see if you can add things to it. Can you find new ideas that, alongside the old ones, will give you an expanded toolbox?

Next time you're out shooting, pay attention to whether you're trying something new or simply applying your "usual tricks" to the subject matter around you. Just the act of thinking about this will help you grow as a photographer.

Shoot first, ask questions later

As photographers, we'll casually throw around the concepts of "shooting" and "post-production." We understand that the process of making a photo occurs in stages. It's strange, then, that we create stress in the field by making opinions about whether we've had any success with our shooting.

The fact is that you don't necessarily know that a photo is good when you shoot it. I am often amazed that I will get home and find that the keeper image from the day's work is one that I never would have thought would amount to anything.

I was recently visiting my parents, and was out shooting. Because it's an area that I'm familiar with, my eyes are kind of dead to it, so I did not expect to get anything. Instead, I was thinking, "I need the camera in my hands. I need to be seeing, I need to be shooting. I need to be practicing. It's fine if I don't come home with anything." True to form, while I was out shooting, I wasn't struck by anything, but I was okay about that. I was practicing, and that felt good.

It's easy in this type of circumstance to get discouraged, so it's important — no matter what you're shooting — to remember, "Hey, I can't tell anything right now. The back of the camera doesn't mean anything. My sense of what's going on doesn't mean anything. I won't know if I've got something until I get home." The point of being out shooting is to be seeing what's around you, and to be in the moment.

Later, after dumping the images into my computer I found a couple of perfectly sturdy images, much better than what I was expecting to come home with.

When you're out shooting, it's easy to get up in your head, for all sorts of different reasons. When that happens, you can become lost, and cease to see photographically. It's important at those moments to not critique your images until you've started your postproduction process.

Remember too, that very often, an image is not finished until you've done some editing, so you often don't know if it's working until you've taken it through your entire workflow. When you reach that point, step back and compose yourself; try to stay focused and be present. Don't get self-critical of your images until you see the final shots. Then you can rip them to shreds as much as you want.

Fill your media card

Here's a simple thing to try, whether you're feeling stuck or not. When you go out to shoot, aim to fill your card.

That's it. Fill the media card in your camera.

Why? When I'm watching students in the field during a workshop, I have noticed that most of the ones who say "I'm not seeing anything today" are the same ones who simply aren't shooting. As you're out prowling around, you should be trying to find things that interest you, things that catch your eye. But at the same time, you need to be regularly looking through the camera, to remind your eye of the process, and because you often need the camera's crop to realize the image.

If you go for a while without shooting, then a feedback system can start. You're possibly not shooting because you're getting afraid of failure. But by not shooting, you're not going to achieve any successes. This fuels your fear of failure and leaves you less likely to shoot. And so on.

So go out and shoot to fill your card.

If you have a big card, it may not be possible to fill it in a single shoot. If you're going out for an hour and your card can hold 2,000 raw files, then you're not going to fill it. But aiming to fill the card will still make this technique work. When I'm working this way I think of it as trying to take a photo about every ten to fifteen seconds.

I'm not saying that quantity equals quality. Quantity does, however, defeat the editor that sits in your head. When you feel like you have a quota to fill, a frequency that you need to maintain, then you're not going to second-guess your impulses. Any play of light, play of geometry, or remotely interesting subject matter — you're going to follow every one of those impulses, just to satisfy that ticking counter that says you need to shoot more. That is the main value of this technique: it doesn't give you time to be self-critical.

Something else this technique does is make you shoot subject matter that you might not normally photograph. If you're out walking around and you've gone twenty seconds without taking a shot and you know you need to get something then you'll find something! Most of it will be crap, but from time to time you'll discover that you've taken a photo of something that's interesting, but which you would never have bothered to shoot before. Desperation can be a great motivator.

This technique is especially fun to try with this extra challenge: Find some place that you feel has little potential, and spend an hour there shooting in this way. Pick an empty lot, a boring industrial park, or some place that you feel you know very well. Go there and aim for 300 photos in an hour.

I'm not advocating that you work this way all the time. There's something to be said for being discerning while shooting, and trying to know what works without having to take a shot. And of course working this way makes for a huge amount of post-production. But it's important to know what this feels like, both because you might find it a good tool to get you out of a stuck place, or a good technique to use on certain kind of shoots, with certain kinds of subject matter. Even if you never work this way again, I guarantee you'll have a fun and interesting time if you at least try it once.

Get into a rut

After "I'm not seeing anything to shoot," the most common complaint I hear from students is, "I'm in a rut." You know the feeling: you're composing all your shots the same way, you're always shooting the same subject matter, you're taking the same picture over and over. You're in a rut. To this, I would say: congratulations! Now try to get into some more.

A while ago, I noticed that, over the course of ten or fifteen years—in different locations and with different subject matter—I often shot the same composition. Certain types of lines and arrangements of lines led me to compose a particular shot. The subject matter was irrelevant; I had to arrange those lines in that specific way. What's curious is that I wasn't aware of how much I was doing it until I noticed how many of these images were in my library. Plainly, I had a rut problem.

Relying on the same compositional ideas can be demoralizing. It can make you feel constrained by your own vision. You feel like a one-trick pony, and that you're lacking in creativity: that a better photographer would find more variety and have a broader vision.

I would offer the idea that you want to get in as many different ruts as you can over the course of your photo career, and here's why. I am now very practiced at shooting a particular composition, which I've inadvertently been re-shooting for years. In fact, I'm not just practiced, I've actually gotten good at this particular, odd skill. That composition is now a piece of my photographic vocabulary. It's something that I can use when I'm building an image, because I know, from practice, that sometimes photos work well when composed in this manner that I've accidentally been practicing.

Just think: what if I'd been in 50 ruts over the course of my life? That would be great! I would have all of these different things that I could fall back on when I encountered a tricky composition. What's more—and I don't know if this will ever really happen—but what if, one day, I come across a situation where the perfect composition for it is to build it in this exact way that I consider to be a rut? Boy, I'm going to be ready for that!

I'm waiting for the day when that happens. And again, if I'd been through 50 other ruts I would have 50 other perfect abilities for the right photographic situation. So, if you feel like you're in a rut, congratulations! Stay with it, keep going, keep shooting that shot, and try to find some other ruts to get into. But don't think of them as ruts. Think of them as practicing a piece of vocabulary that will be valuable to you in the future.

Making choices

Every summer I have the good fortune of teaching photography to a class full of skilled teenagers. If there's a single way that I can describe their work, it's that it has a purity that I wish I could return to. Not a purity of content, but a purity in approach. None of these students are shooting for a living — most are not even worried about whether they can "turn photography into something." They're simply shooting because they're interested in what they see in the frame and what they can do with that.

Still, they are young and mostly inexperienced. At the longest, they've only been shooting for three or four years, so they still have much to learn, and because few have had any formal photography education, there are often gaps in their knowledge. So I can be surprised when, during a critique session, the students almost always have answers to the questions we pose. If we ask, "Why did you position this here?" or, "Why did you choose to render this in black and white?" or, "Did you choose shallow depth of field or was that a mistake?" they almost always have an answer. And in most cases, it's a well-reasoned answer, even if it doesn't necessarily lead to the best result.

The reason this impresses me is because these people are young. They're at an age when they're accustomed to having an authority figure tell them what to do and when. Yet when it comes to creative process they understand and respect the fundamental driving force of all creativity: making choices.

The process of taking a photo is no different than any other creative process in that it is simply a progression through a long series of choices: How to frame, how much depth of field, how much motion stopping, how much contrast, how dark are the shadows, how light are the highlights, what's the photo about, what's the mood, what's the overall tone, which lines should intersect, where should the horizon be, and on and on.

None of those questions seem like incisive, awe-inspiring, important questions, yet each one is critical to getting a good result. If you skip any of them, or if you don't fully commit to your decision about any of them, it can show in your final image. If you're in the field and are finding that you aren't getting anywhere with what you're trying to shoot, ask yourself if you're making choices. A lot of times you might be waiting for the situation to force your hand, rather than taking charge of your process and committing to strong choices.

I hate making decisions. I hate choosing what to eat, what book to read next, what movie to watch. There's rarely a price to pay for this — waffling, hedging and procrastinating on any of those decisions simply wastes time. Hedging on your creative decisions, though, weakens your work. When it comes to taking photos, even a bad decision, fully committed, is better than no decision — accepting something by default. If teenagers at the start of their photographic journey can understand that, so can the rest of us.

Work with your eyes, not your brain

I was riding my motorcycle out of Monument Valley in northern Arizona, and the sun had mostly gone down. All of a sudden, the sun lit up the one monument in the area. And then, I made a mistake: I decided that I didn't have enough time to shoot it, and so should just enjoy it. As I rode along, the light stayed beautiful until I finally decided I had to shoot it. But I'd wasted too much time — even as I pulled over and tried to get out of my helmet, I could tell that the best light had already passed.

With the light changing quickly I didn't feel like I had time to get my camera out, so I pulled out my iPhone. Through it all I had imagined shooting the spectacularly lit rock feature, previsualizing a specific photo. Now that my procrastination had relegated me to shooting with my phone, I was stuck with a lens that was too wide. My subject was too small in the frame and the image seemed to be much more about the road. It took a moment for me to let go of the image that was in my head, but the fading light kicked me into gear.

While it's sometimes important to have a vision of the shot that you want, it's also important to not let that visualization blind you to what's actually in front of you. Because of limitations of time and gear, I couldn't take the image I wanted — it appeared that the best I could do was to take a picture of pavement. So that's what I did. Once I'd embraced that I found I had a lot of nice things to work with — receding parallel lines, a spectacular geological wonder in the background, some nice light, approaching cars. I finally ended up with a shot that I was happy with.

Sometimes, you have to throw out the whole vision thing in order to see.

Always be a photographer

We take photos for many reasons. Sometimes we're practicing "serious" photography and at other times we're simply documenting our world and taking snapshots. If you're like me, you often keep a dividing line between those two photographic realms; they almost become different disciplines. Sometimes, if I'm out with some friends and there's an opportunity to take a snapshot, I don't actually do the work of a photographer. I just grab a quick picture. When I get home and see my rather ordinary-looking snapshot I find myself frustrated because, the fact is, there's no reason not to always be a good photographer. You can bring your photographic skill set to bear on any image.

For example, I was motorcycling through Death Valley and got to a place that I really like — and my butt was ready to get off the bike for a while. When you're on a bike trip, you tend to take a lot of pictures of your motorcycle. Sometimes this is simply because you're excited to be out on your bike; other times it's because it is the only thing around. But also, I like to document the ride as I go. So I grabbed the camera and took a shot of my bike.

What I got was the bike and the location. It is an incredibly boring photograph. As I was heading to the bike to get back on it, I came to my senses and realized that I should take a real picture of what was going on. I needed to do the work of a photographer and so started working the shot.

I tried a few different ideas, looking for relationships between the bike's geometry and the geometry of the landscape. It took a few frames to finesse some details and get all the lines intersecting in ways I was comfortable with, but in the process I went very quickly from a snapshot to a finished image which not only gave me a cooler shot of the bike, but a much nicer shot of Death Valley as well. At the most basic level, my final shot worked better than the first because I had a more clearly defined subject, which related nicely with the background.

There's no reason not to do this kind of thing on every picture that you shoot. I don't mean that anytime someone wants a snapshot you have to shoot two dozen frames, but you can think about some simple things. For example, if you're taking a snapshot of some friends, are they standing in harsh lighting? If so, move them into some shade. Can you simplify the background somehow? Can you come up with a composition that isn't just people standing in front of some thing?

Trying to move quickly through these decisions, without annoying your friends, is a great exercise itself and good training for shooting in fast-moving environments. With just a little bit of extra effort, not only will you get better snapshots, you'll get a chance to practice.

"Pretty" photos matter

As photographers, we all sit with a long legacy of strong and powerful photojournalism, and a history of important photos.

Most of us like to feel that something we do in our life matters in some fashion, that we're somehow contributing to society. Sometimes, when you're out taking a photo of, say, a dead leaf on the sidewalk, it can be hard not to question whether what you're doing is a good use of your time. If you're like me, then you might sometimes wonder why you're simply taking a "pretty" picture when you could be using your camera to serve a cause or tell an important story.

My friend Robert Zakanitch is a painter and one of the founders of the Pattern and Decorative Movement. Amongst other things, the P&D movement developed in response to an art world that found "decorative" or "pretty" work to be irrelevant and unimportant. (**cdp.pub/decorative**)

One day I made a crack about some image of mine being "merely pretty" and immediately got a strong earful from Zakanitch. Creating something pretty, he said, is an act of civility, and being civil is the cornerstone of civilization. Therefore, when you create something pretty you are strengthening civilization itself. I found this to be a comforting argument and stuck it away in the back of my head, figuring I could trot it out for myself the next time I was wondering if shooting a pretty picture was a waste of time.

A few weeks later, I came to truly understand what he had been talking about. I had traveled to South Africa to work with a friend on a project that involved shooting older South African women in their homes in the sprawling township of Khayelitsha. These were women who were old enough that they had grown up in the era before the entire black population of the country was forcibly relocated into what are, essentially, shanty towns. As we visited more of these homes, one thing became conspicuous. In every place that we went, even structures where the elements freely blew through a 2-inch gap between the walls and the ceiling, there was a lace doily on the rickety coffee table, or a tea set on a shelf, or a stack of place mats on a ramshackle counter.

All of these women were living with limited resources, and every one of them worked to ensure that their homes had at least some level of civility, as measured by the standards they had learned before apartheid. These simple pretty things help them maintain their dignity, sense of self, and sense of purpose as they continue to fight against being marginalized.

What this experience drove home for me was that Zakanitch was right. There are no "merely pretty" acts, or photos. Making a well-crafted, beautiful image is an act of civility. It strengthens and defines our civilization. Don't ever hesitate to do it.

Shoot sketches

Photography is the only visual art medium that allows you to produce a technically perfect result every time — assuming that you're doing things well. Even if your photo is poorly composed, you can still get an image with good exposure, proper focus, good color and great tone. In other words, your camera usually produces what looks like a finished work, even if your concept was off.

While it's great that the camera provides you automatically with so much, the fact that every shot looks like a finished project can set you up for unrealistic expectations. The odd reality of photography is that, if you're doing your job in the right way, then most of what you shoot will be bad, reject images.

To understand why, think about how a fine art painter works. It's the rare painter who sits at the canvas and paints a finished product in a single pass, starting from nothing. Most painters start with sketches and studies. Sometimes they'll work on their sketches, studies and ideas for months or years before they feel comfortable and confident enough to start on a painting. (Even those painters who don't sketch beforehand usually repeatedly rework areas on the canvas, replacing and refining ideas as they try to find their way to a finished result.) You would never walk into a painter's studio, see 15 sketches on the floor, and one finished painting, and say "Wow, you only got one out of 16—that's a pretty lousy ratio."

Very often, what makes a good photographer a good photographer is that they have a lousy shooting ratio: they understand the importance of sketching. They know that their initial idea and vision of an image probably isn't the best one, so they work their shots. They experiment and explore, moving about and refining their idea as they shoot more and more. Each one of those refinements and ideas is the equivalent of a sketch. Sometimes they hit the best idea and then keep going, continuing to sketch in search of something different.

When they get home, they might have had a shooting ratio of 50:1; 50 different experiments and options to get a single keeper image. And if they come home with four keeper images at a ratio of 50:1 then that means they like four out of 200 images. And they are able to work this way because they're comfortable with the idea that this is how the process is supposed to go.

None of us likes to feel like a bad photographer, but the medium is set up to make us feel that way, because every image looks like a finished product. So when you've only got four keepers out of 200, and those 200 look like finished photos, it's hard not to feel like you're doing something wrong. You're not. Photography, like every other creative process, requires iterations, and just because each iteration looks finished doesn't mean that it is.

Work your shots, experiment and explore, and try to think of those explorations as sketches. Look at those extreme shooting ratios as a sign that you're doing things right. Effective photographers mostly take images that need to be thrown away.

MIND GAMES

The professional tennis world is divided into separate organizations for men and women, each with their own variations on the rules. In most professional men's tournaments, from the moment they step onto the court, the players are not allowed to communicate with anyone. In some women's tournaments, players are allowed a brief consult with someone during a changeover (the break every other game, when players change sides). Lately, thanks to fancy microphones, tennis broadcasts have sometimes included audio of the discussions between female players and whoever it is they're consulting.

It's surprising to see how often the person the player chooses to talk to is not a coach who will make suggestions of strategy or tactics, but a sports psychologist who will try to help the player get out of their head and back into the game. Most of the time, these conversations run along the lines of "remember, you want this, you've always wanted this more than anything, and you're capable of getting it" and so on.

I bring this up to illustrate that everyone, in a variety of fields and disciplines, knows those voices that zap your confidence or tell you that you're not doing a good job or that you're wasting your time and so on and so forth. Sometimes the voices act up because you're feeling insecure about your technical ability, sometimes they pile on to tear down your self-esteem and sense of aesthetic. When they're really going, they can hit you at an existential level and lead you to question the purpose of the practice of photography.

In this section we're going to examine some of the things your brain can say to you that can get in the way of you not only developing as a photographer but of shooting at all. In some cases I'll present suggestions for how you might short-circuit these modes of thought. For times when I don't, I'm hoping that acknowledging the problem will at least help you understand that those things you're saying to yourself are not necessarily uncommon.

Am I good?

Who cares?

Of the many nagging voices that your brain can produce while you're shooting, perhaps the most damaging and pointless is the one that asks "Am I good at this?" You might not use these exact words; you might have a variation of them, but whatever the wording, the simple answer "who cares" can short-circuit this question.

Why does it matter if you're any good? The question of "good" implies that you're on some kind of linear path and that at the end of that path is "best." Let's clear that up right away: there is no "best photographer." There is no single, great, end-of-the-road that you can arrive at that indicates that you have learned everything you can learn. There have been hundreds of great photographers throughout the history of photography, but the "best photographer" simply doesn't exist.

Asking the question, "Am I good?" implies a destination—a level of accomplishment—and you shouldn't have a destination in mind as you pursue your photographic career. You should be shooting because you enjoy shooting. Maybe you enjoy it because you feel there is something you can reveal to the world by expressing it photographically. Maybe you like the process of arranging things inside a frame. Or maybe it doesn't make you feel anything other than a sense of calm or contentment. Or perhaps it's any combination of these things, or a different thing entirely.

Creativity is not a competition. There are no winners and losers, and there is no "best."

There can, of course, be better, and that might be what this question is really asking. There's absolutely nothing wrong with wanting to improve, as long as you know that there's no end to this process of improvement.

Why am I so fixated on demolishing the idea of a destination? Because it's a distraction, and because it runs counter to the idea of photography as a practice. If you're serious about photography, then you're in it for the long haul. Yes, you want to improve, and measuring progress is an important component of improving, but the essence of practice is to accept that you are on a journey, and to be present and committed to where you are on your path at that particular moment. Good or bad doesn't matter, because you are where you are.

Why do other people's photos look better than mine?

If you've ever been in a photo class you might have noticed that the person sitting next to you always seems to have better photos than you do. Of course, this might be because that person *is* a better photographer than you are, but more often I think it's because their work looks fresh to you. Our own work always looks a little stale because it has to compete with what's going on inside our head.

What we bring to a photo as a viewer is as important to our appreciation of that image as what the photographer put into it while shooting. This is especially true when it comes to looking at our own work. We view our own photos alongside the images of the original scene that remain in our head, as well as our expectations of what we thought the photo could be. We even compare our own photos to other senses. Perhaps the photo is of an event that made you very happy and so you have happy associations of that moment. If you don't regain that emotion when you look at your photo, you can be left feeling wanting. For any number of reasons, our own images are often disappointing.

Learning how to evaluate your own images is a skill that is as important as learning how to evaluate the work of others. I can't give you a foolproof way to do this, but I can give you one suggestion that will make it easier to be fair to your own images: set them aside. After processing your images into a state that you like, move on to something else and leave them alone for a few months so that you can return to them later with fresh eyes. This is the simplest way to try to see your images as other people might see them. As an experiment, take yourself on a shoot and when you come back, don't look at any of your images. Copy them to a drive, forget about them, and come back to them in six months. You might find that delaying your review is a way that you prefer to work, when you can.

What the passage of time can do is lessen the images and feelings that are in your head — those feelings that few photos can bear comparison to. Returning to photos after a few months will very often give you an honest perspective that you can't get when the original scenes are still fresh in your mind.

Even if you've got a set of photos that you feel good about, it's worth returning to it after a few months, or years, and evaluating the original shoot again. You might be surprised to discover that there are some images that you hadn't recognized as keepers when you first passed through them. This can happen for a few reasons. Sometimes the image doesn't compare to what you thought it would be, and when you've forgotten that expectation you can judge the photo more fairly. At other times, it might be that you're in the middle of a photographic growth spurt. When you shot the image you had a flash of a newer aesthetic, but couldn't hang on to it until you got home. Months later, maybe after that aesthetic has developed more, you are able to recognize the image for the more sophisticated creation that it is.

Early in your career, it's easy to feel rushed, to push and hurry to try to build a body of work. But it's going to take time. There are no shortcuts, so do your best to build good work, rather than to set a pace. Doing your best work might mean waiting before sending your images through post-production.

Fear

You cannot make yourself immune to fear; it will always be a part of your life. It will also always be a part of your photographic life. Fear of what? Fear of not liking your work, fear of feeling like a bad photographer, fear of critique, fear you're not getting better, and on and on.

While you can't make yourself immune to these fears, can change your reaction to fear itself, and alter your relationship to fear so that it doesn't hamper your creative process.

Most people have the same reflexive response to feeling fear: they try to control the future. Because if you can control the future, then you may be able to change things so that whatever it is that you fear can't happen. And for most people, the best mechanism that they have for controlling the future is the word "no."

"Do you want to go skydiving?"
"No."

And there, the future has been successfully controlled to preclude you from meeting your demise in a skydiving accident.

What's tricky about "no" is that you have many ways of saying it, and some of them are subtle. Therefore, in addition to looking out for the word "no" when you feel fear, you need to look for whether your response to a situation is actually an attempt to control the future.

For example: you've been out shooting all day and you haven't yet gotten anything that you're excited about. You're now starting to become more critical of your ideas, and so you're shooting less. You're likely doing this because, with each additional image you shoot, your feel your hit ratio getting worse. From past experience you know that when you arrive home with a bunch of images and you don't like most of them, you feel bad, so now it feels safer to be zero for 20 instead of zero for 40.

In other words, you are choosing not to shoot because you're worried about how you'll feel about the results later. This is a form of saying no. You're saying no to the impulse you're having right now to ensure that you won't feel bad when you get home.

You'll often hear people express the idea that the key to artistic success (and general happiness) is to "stay present" and "be in the moment." That's great advice, but it doesn't include any hint about how to achieve that state. Recognizing you're saying "no" is often the key to staying present, because "no" is often an attempt to control your future prospects, rather than your current situation.

When a photographic impulse hits, that's a gift. If you say yes to it, you're in the moment. Even if the initial idea isn't great, following it and working your scene might lead to something that is great. If, instead, you start to question how the image fits into a shooting ratio, or whether it's a cliché or how it compares to what anyone else is shooting — now you're no longer present. Now you're thinking about how you're going to feel when you review the image in the future. Those questions have nothing to do with the moment, nothing to do with the initial impulse, and nothing to do with the process of photography. They are a fear-based attempt to control how you will feel in the future.

If you say yes and take the shot anyway, you might still feel lousy when you get home, but that's something to deal with then. What will make you a better photographer is continuing to shoot now. There is no path in life that will guarantee you a comfortable future so you might as well stop trying to find one. Feel your fear, acknowledge it, then give up your desire to control it, say yes to your ideas and photographic process, and get back to work.

Clichés

"That's a cliché," is something my brain frequently likes to whisper to me as I have framed a shot.

By "cliché," what it means is that a lot of people (possibly including me) have already taken the shot. Not even necessarily that exact, specific photograph, but the same type of subject matter in the same composition.

These statements are, of course, expressions of the fear that I'm not being original. Lack of originality is such a common creative problem that we actually have clichés about it: "There are no new ideas," or "There are only seven different kinds of stories," and whatnot.

After millennia of humans being creative, and after almost 200 years of people making photos, the idea that we can be original seems pretty silly to me. After all that time, of course there will be repetition. Take a look at the *insta_repeat* account on Instagram, to see a fascinating display of many different people taking exactly the same photo (**cdp.pub/cliche**).

So, what do you do when your brain starts nagging you about originality? As with so many of the other ways it tries to trip you up, you can answer it very quickly with "So what?" and then take the photo anyway. If that's not a strong enough solution for you, then consider some of these ideas.

First, if you have had an impulse to take a photo, that is a gift — a luxury. I expect that you've had the experience of spending a day out walking and not seeing anything — not having any impulses to take a picture. So, when you get one, by god, follow that process and finish that photo, because you were lucky to have gotten that in the first place!

Second, during that process of going and shooting that clichéd photo that everyone else has already taken, you're still going to solve problems. You're still going to go through the mechanical process of taking a picture, and that process is still valuable practice.

The potential danger here is that, instead of going home feeling bad because you didn't see anything, you're going to go home and feel bad because all you saw was a cliché. If that happens, then consider this: the reason an image is a cliché is because that particular arrangement of things that you saw has resonance for you. It's so resonant that lots and lots of people see it. That's good news! You are so in touch with the baseline of human visual sense, the aesthetic, and the current zeitgeist in photography that you can recognize the same thing that everyone else does. Wouldn't it be worse if you didn't see that clichéd photo?

Recognizing a cliché does not mean you're a bad photographer, it means that you're actually, at some level, in the groove that you need to be in, because it's the groove that lots of other people are going to recognize as a good photograph.

Does all this mean that you need to take the same photos as everyone else? Of course not, and if you ask yourself that question you've gone off the deep end of overthinking. Stop worrying about all this, see the cliché, do the work, take the shot. You don't have to show it to anybody else. Maybe you will build on that cliché and find something that no one else has found before and come out with an image that is not a cliché. Probably not, but you never know, and there's no harm in trying.

Maybe it's not a cliché

Some images definitely are clichés — a line of brightly colored boat prows in a harbor, a back-lit smoker in a busy café, an ancient barn in the country. Sometimes, though, your cliché alarm can go off prematurely, especially if you're a less-experienced photographer who hasn't looked at a lot of photographs.

The human visual system is more neurological than optical. Up to a point, we see what we expect to see in the world, not what's actually there. What that means for a photographer is twofold. One, it means that you may not recognize shots that are out there because you simply don't see them. Two, it means that the shots that you do see feel obvious to you, and so you assume that everyone else sees them also. Sometimes what you see as a cliché only feels that way because you can't imagine not recognizing that scene as a photo.

It can be very hard to allow yourself the possibility of having a unique vision. Let's face it, even thinking such a thing feels conceited. It's important to understand that when I say "unique vision," I don't mean that you've necessarily spotted a great photograph, just that you've spotted something that other people might not.

I tell you this simply to reinforce the idea that, during those times when your brain is trying to talk you out of shooting something, shoot it anyway. Maybe you're right. Maybe it is a boring, cliché-ridden, obvious picture, but maybe it's not. Maybe it is a photograph that you see that others wouldn't recognize. Take it home, work it up, show it to some people, and see what their response is. As you move through the world, following your vision, and paying attention to the vision of other photographers, you may find that there is a place for you, a place that you weren't able to recognize before.

Don't control the shoot before you start

You've got an afternoon available, and you've decided you want to go out and take some pictures. You pack a bag full of gear, you get yourself ready to go, and then you face the problem of deciding where.

In San Francisco, I have plenty of options. I can go to the ocean, bicycle to North Beach, the Italian neighborhood, or walk to Chinatown. I could go out to the piers in the industrial area, or prowl about a recovered wetland. All this choice often leaves me frozen, and so I'll stand in my apartment and pace in a circle and try to figure out where I should go by imagining what photos I'm going to take in any of those locations. When I can't imagine anything, I decide that there's nowhere I want to shoot.

I should say that I don't just do this in San Francisco. I can do this anywhere that I'm considering taking a photo walk.

The reason I get stuck is because I'm demanding control. I'm trying to guarantee that I'm going to come back with a good picture. And so I want to somehow find a calculus that will explain which of these different destinations is going to guarantee a good result, because I hate the idea of coming back with bad images. And so I sit and think: "I don't know what I'd shoot in Chinatown. I can't imagine a single photo there. Nope, can't think of anything at the beach, either." And on and on.

The problem is, the questions I'm asking are ridiculous. Of course I can't visualize any photos in those locations — I'm not at those locations. Photography is not something that you plan ahead for, unless it's a situation where you've recognized the potential shot and thought, "Oh, I should come back here later when the light is good." Trying to imagine the images before you go is an indication that you've fallen into a place of profound insecurity. You are feeling insecure about whether you're going to come back with good images or not.

At that point, what I do sometimes is actually roll dice. I assign locations to the numbers and let chance decide and then I go there. Since I've already decided that all possible locations are dead-ends, then one is as good as any other.

The important thing to remember here is that the problem is not my destinations; the problem is my insecurity-fueled desire to guarantee a good outcome. You can rarely talk yourself out of insecurity, so you must find ways to make yourself act. Trust in the process and the fact that, most of the time, the practice of shooting will get you out of your head and back on your photographic feet.

"What if I'm stupid?"

Years ago I had a computer programming project and I bought a programming book by Aaron Hilligass. The book was very good; he is definitely a great teacher.

In the introduction, he included this section called "How to Learn":

"While learning something new, many students will think, 'Damn, this is hard for me. I wonder if I am stupid.' Because stupidity is such an unthinkable terrible thing in our culture, the students will then spend hours constructing arguments that explain why they are intelligent yet are having difficulties. The moment you start down this path, you have lost your focus.

"I used to have a boss named Rock. Rock had earned a degree in astrophysics from Cal Tech and had never had a job in which he used his knowledge of the heavens. Once I asked him whether he regretted getting the degree. "Actually, my degree in astrophysics has proven to be very valuable," he said. "Some things in this world are just hard. When I am struggling with something, I sometimes think 'Damn, this is hard for me. I wonder if I'm stupid,' and then I remember that I have a degree in astrophysics from Caltech; I must not be stupid."

I see this with photo students. Whatever it is they're trying to learn, they get worried that "Maybe I'm not good enough to learn this, maybe I'm not smart enough. Maybe I don't have natural photographic talent."

As soon as they're off in that realm, they've stopped dealing with the actual problem at hand. So I'm going to remind you right now that learning photography is difficult. It's okay to have a hard time with it, it's okay to be intimidated by it, it's okay to fail at it, over and over and over. In some cases, you're simply not going to understand some of it, and that's OK, too. You can learn to work around those things, and in fact, workarounds might lead you to forms of innovation.

You work with what you have. Maybe you're not great at post-production, but you're a fantastic shooter. That's OK. You can either find someone who is good at post-production and collaborate with them, or you can learn to work within those limitations to arrive at a place that you had never foreseen in the first place. All of this worry, all of this intimidation, it doesn't get you anywhere. But most importantly, it distracts from the tasks that can get you somewhere. You can do yourself and your process a great benefit by trying to recognize and identify any of your own intimidation-based roadblocks. Once you see them, you might have an easier time avoiding them.

Things going wrong can be good news

There are many ways that you can have your confidence shaken while you're shooting. One of them happens when photos don't match what you had in your mind's eye. Of course, no one else knows what was in your mind's eye — they judge the work on its own, but this can be difficult for you to do. Lately, I've come to realize that when my shooting is not going to my satisfaction, I feel an odd sense of relief.

Making a great photo is incredibly difficult, and it doesn't happen that often even for the best photographers. I can remember taking photos when I was younger and confidently thinking that I'd nailed the shot. Now when I look at those images I think "well, this is just lousy." What's changed is that I now have a better sense of the difference between a photo that works and one that doesn't. So when things aren't going well, it's actually a relief to me that I know they're not going well. Getting proof that I can recognize that my work isn't up to snuff can actually be a confidence builder because it's proof that my experience has led me to a stronger aesthetic and a better ability to evaluate the quality of my work as I shoot.

So if you're having a difficult time, if you're feeling like everything you shoot is turning out badly, it might actually mean that you're on the right track. You're holding yourself to a standard; you're setting a goal that is high and that's where you want it to be to do good work. You don't have to be hypercritical, that's not what I'm saying. Nor should you think that hating your images is a sign of progress or advancement. Rather, I'm saying that your assessment of your own work is going to be affected as your aesthetic matures.

Knowing the difference between a good photo and a bad photo — even if it's a bad photo that you've taken — is a great asset for a photographer, and it means you'll be more likely to find and get the good one when it comes along.

Take the "why not" shot

Once, on a video shoot at a remote farmhouse, I was waiting for the crew to finish rigging something. I found myself noticing the roofline of the house, and a small weathervane that was mounted there. I started to take some photos of it, and came up with some nice silhouettes, which I liked just fine. I didn't expect that I would do anything with them, but I was at least shooting. Then I went into my head.

"I'm taking pictures of a roof," I thought.

After that came, "is this a dumb thing to be taking a picture of?"

So, I stopped.

We have all sorts of ways to talk ourselves out of taking photos. "Why am I taking this? It's a cliché.... I've already got images like this.... It's boring."

I was teaching a workshop with the photographer Keith Carter when one of these questions came up. Keith had a very simple answer: "Why not?" For some reason, those words stuck in my head. For the photographer, I think there's a lot of power in them.

I got out of the roofline situation by using those two simple words. When I went into my head and started thinking "I'm taking pictures of a rooftop, why?" I answered, "Why not? Why not take this picture? Why not, if nothing else, get the practice? Why not explore this scene? Why not allow the opportunity to notice something on the roof that I hadn't noticed before? Why not take the risk on there being a picture there that I couldn't have imagined? Why not take the risk of coming home and not liking the picture, but being able to say, 'Well, at least I tried.'"

I have been clear in telling you that your goal as a photographer is not to take great photos. Your goal is to practice. If you are serious about committing to the idea of being a practicing photographer, then following any impulse to shoot is a worthwhile endeavor, as long as you stay engaged with your visual sense and the world around you, doing the work of a photographer. You never know what you're going to end up back at home with. So, why not?

Passion and boredom

We love our myths about artists. We like our painters to be crazy and our jazz musicians to be drug addicts and our writers to struggle with alcohol and suicide. Most of all, we want our artists to be passionate. We want them to be people who have to create to survive, and whose first and last thoughts each day are about their love for their craft.

Personally, I think selling this idea of "overwhelming passion" is a mistake. Setting aside the fact that the word "passion" stems from the Latin word for suffering, the problem with saying that you require passion to effectively pursue something is that it's simply not true. If you're the type of person who isn't predisposed toward feeling an all-consuming drive for something, then being told that you have to have passion for something can leave you feeling like you have an extra obstacle to overcome.

The fact is, passion is not required to be good at something. Dedication and hard work are required, but you don't have to have an all-consuming urge, or even sense of enjoyment to have dedication and drive.

I'm not knocking the people who are passionate about one thing or another; I *am* trying to let you know that you don't have to worry if you can't relate to the feelings they express about their pursuit. What's more, I'd like to let you off the hook about a few other things.

First of all, you don't have to like every aspect of photography. I often find shooting to be a tedious chore that I have to wade through to get to the thing that I really enjoy, which is editing and printing. I know other people who feel the exact opposite — every minute they have to sit in front of the computer is torture, because it takes away shooting time. Dorothy Parker famously said "I hate writing, but I love having written"—perhaps the most extreme version of not liking part of a creative process.

Don't be afraid of fessing up to your feelings about one part of the process or another. You need to know if there's a part of the process that you're resistant to, because that resistance might be hampering you. It might be necessary for you to contrive mechanisms to help encourage you through the parts of photographic process that you don't like as much.

Second: it's okay to get bored with photography. It happens to me, and I'm sure it happens to other people, but few of us ever talk about it, most likely because we're worried about not looking passionate. It is also possible that we are afraid that becoming bored means that we are not true photographers. Don't worry, you can get bored with anything.

There's a big world full of lots of fascinating stuff out there. You can get bored with photography because something else interesting has caught your eye, or because you've been doing it so much you feel like you're in a rut, or because you've plateaued and advancing beyond that is hard, or because repetition is ultimately boring. So chill out — it's okay to get bored with a creative endeavor. It doesn't mean you're not a creative person.

As for what to do about it, I think you follow the boredom. Don't fight it, don't try to deny it, don't try to talk yourself out of it, and certainly don't worry about it. Do what you do when you're bored with anything else: stop doing it. Walking away from it might present a new fear, the fear that your interest might not ever come back. But I think if you're far enough into photography that you're reading a book of essays like this one, then you don't need to worry about your underlying interest level.

In the face of phone addiction, there's been a lot of research recently into "micro-boredom," a state of mind that we used to enter into regularly, but that we don't anymore because we reach for our phones as soon as we feel it. Researchers have learned that boredom is actually a necessary part of the creative process. As a muscle needs to relax after flexing, your brain seems to have similar needs. Boredom might be nothing more than your brain saying it needs to recharge. That's why you don't need to worry. If you've stuck with it this long, your camera will call you again.

What's worse is to continue to work while you're bored, for the simple reason that you won't enjoy it. Do that enough and you will begin to associate photography with lack of enjoyment.

Boredom is going to wax and wane. You're going to come in and out of it. The worst thing you can do is make it worse by worrying about it. Don't worry about it. Everybody gets bored with the photographic process. It's perfectly normal. Just go with it.

POST-PRODUCTION

Though you may not know it by name, you most likely have heard Bach's Suite for Cello No 1 in G Major, the first of his unaccompanied cello suites. It's been used in movies, TV shows and commercials and, when played well, is a spectacular piece of music.

It begins with a repeating motif that starts on a low G. What's interesting about that low G is that, on a cello, it's played on an open string. An open string is one that doesn't have a finger pressing on it, and so open strings always have a longer reverberation than a fingered string.

As a cellist, when you play this piece, you immediately discover the great gift that Bach left for you in the form of that open string. While composing, he was thinking ahead to the particulars of the instrument, and he recognized that repeating a pulse on that open string would create a constant resonant tone underneath all of the other notes. It's a great example of a composer intimately understanding the idiomatic particulars of the instrument he was writing for, long before he could hear the music played.

As photographers, we regularly engage in a similar process. We shoot images in particular ways because we know that we can process them in particular ways. We shoot with the expectation of what will happen to the image later, through adjustments, curation and presentation. In fact, while shooting, if you don't have one eye in the darkroom — be it a digital or wet darkroom — then you're likely not taking full advantage of your medium.

Like all other aspects of photography, post-production requires practice, both technical and aesthetic. In this section, we'll look at how to add post-production practice to your regimen.

Less is more

I regularly teach a photo workshop in a program that includes eight other artistic disciplines. One day, during lunch at one of these workshops, the poet George Bilgere came up to me and asked, "Can I bring my students into your class today? They've been in the library all week and are starting to go mad." I told him that we were doing a critique session at a particular time and he agreed that might be interesting.

Of course, these days everyone is a photographer, so the poets were quite interested in the hour's worth of critiques that they watched.

That night at dinner, George told me, "It's fascinating — you were saying the same things during your photo critique that I say when I'm critiquing a poem: 'You don't need this,' 'this is extra,' 'this serves no purpose,' 'what are you trying to say with this bit?'"

I found two things interesting about this. First, creative process is creative process. It doesn't matter what discipline you practice. Sure, musicians and dancers have an athletic component that most photographers don't have to concern themselves with, but they still have to solve most of the same creative problems that we have to solve with photos. It can be inspiring and informative to look at how other disciplines identify and address the same kinds of problems that we face when creating images.

Second, most of the critique points that George listed fall into the "less is more" category. I've always assumed that photographers suffer from "too much" more than other disciplines, so it was fascinating to hear him zero in on that particular point.

"Less is more" is a cliché, of course, but it's probably the most important, most helpful cliché that you can follow if you want to improve your photography. Without a doubt, the suggestions I make the most when critiquing images are suggestions of elimination. Eliminating content, eliminating color, lessening the strength of an edit, hiding something through vignetting or tonal adjustment, and so on.

Why is "less" such an effective guideline to follow? In photography, one reason is because photographers start out with so much. A painter starts with a blank canvas, we start with the entire world. Even a simple landscape shot can be cluttered with all sorts of extra visual elements. Maybe there's a line of telephone poles in the distance, or a discolored patch of grass, or a dried-up watering hole. When you first point your camera at the scene, your default framing might include all of those things. Does that mean they all need to be included?

Quite often the difficult work of composition and exposure choice has to do with trying to figure out how to eliminate something from the frame.

But I think the real power of "less" has to do with engagement. When you choose to show less you're asking the viewer — or reader or audience member — to do more. Rather than showing them everything, you're guiding their awareness to a point, and letting them do the rest of the work. That bit that they do on their own is invested with something of themselves, and that very often is the bit that gives them an attachment to the work.

To fully embrace the idea of "less" is an exercise in eliminating some of your ego. It means accepting that the viewer is a creative partner and that you can't make them have the exact same experience that you had. It's allowing for the possibility that they can have a better experience than you had, because they can project their own feelings, experiences and associations into the image, to create a result with deep meaning for them. The less you include in the photo, the greater the chance that they'll have the opportunity to make those projections.

Be ruthless to your photos. It's better to have left something out than to have included too much. Trust your audience.

Editing vs. editing

Before the dawn of the digital age of photography, "editing" meant the process of reviewing the images from a shoot to select the ones that you wanted printed. These days, when we say "editing" we usually mean "image editing," the process of adjusting, retouching and performing other post-production tasks. You still go through that old-school editing process, of course — just like film photographers, you don't take every single image through a post-production process, but few people think of image selection as something they need to practice. The fact is, though, editing a set of images down to only the best ones is itself a skill.

Obviously, when you're making selects, you aim to choose "the good pictures." These are the ones that have the best aesthetic qualities and are free from technical problems such as soft focus, lens flares, and so on. These images aren't always finished — they might require post-production to achieve the look you envisioned when you took the shot. But with experience you'll be able to recognize images that can be completed in post-production.

All of that is the easy part of choosing selects. At some point, it's very likely that you're going to be asked to deliver a specific number of images. Perhaps this is because a teacher in a class has asked you to submit some images for a critique. Or maybe a photo contest or application to a gallery requires you to submit a specific number of images. This is when things can become more difficult.

Here are some suggestions for how to improve your ability to make selects when evaluating your images, especially as you build your practice:

- **Don't delete images.** No matter how much time you spend reviewing, there will be images that you overlook. If you delete those images, you'll never have a second chance at them. I can think of a number of shots of my own that I didn't recognize as keepers until years later. Sure, if it's wildly out of focus or your finger is in front of the camera, there's probably no reason to keep it. But keep everything that doesn't have horrible technical flaws and use your browsing software to mark the ones you like. The unmarked ones might yield a keeper later.
- **Make your first pass a quick one.** Overanalysis is the surest way to get lost in the weeds when editing your images. For your first pass,

move quickly. Try not to think too much. Let yourself have a quick, visceral response to the images. If you find yourself wavering at all, mark those wavery images and return to them later. Once you've grabbed the low-hanging fruit, you can make additional passes to dig a little deeper.

- **When in doubt, walk away.** I've watched many students spend lots of time flipping back and forth between two images, trying to decide which they like better. When you're really stuck, put those images away. Come back to them tomorrow and see if you have a more immediate response. Often, fresh eyes are all it takes to make a choice.

- **Follow directions.** I'm often amazed when, after asking students to each give me three images, someone gives me five and then offers up the excuse "I couldn't decide." When someone gives you instructions for a specific set of images, not being able to decide is not an option. What you're really saying is "I want you to do my work for me," and I guarantee that few people want to hear that.

When asked to select a specific number of images, most people fall down in making the very final selects. They might start with 30 candidates and quickly get it down to ten, but then get stuck winnowing that down to, say, three.

The easiest way to make those very final cuts is with a process of elimination. Start by asking if any two images are similar — similar in composition, similar in content, similar in color palette, similar in field of view. Now decide which of those two is best and throw out the other. Of the remaining images, see if you now notice any similarities. Very often simply looking for similar pairs will make it easy to eliminate the last two or three photos that you need to get rid of.

If you don't see similarities find other criteria that you can use to eliminate images: "This is the only image with a person in it"; "This is the only black and white image"; "This is the only portrait-oriented image." Observations like that can make it easier to find images that don't fit as well into your set of selections.

The mistake that some people make when trying to refine a set of edits is that they focus on trying to figure out what they like. In many cases, it's much easier to figure out what you don't like. That's why process of elimination can be such a powerful tool. Don't look for good stuff, look for bad stuff or stuff that doesn't fit.

Learning to make selects is another aspect of your aesthetic and your ability to see, which means this process will get easier with practice. Also, with experience, you will learn to not treat your images with as much preciousness. With experience, you'll be more willing to kill off images, because you'll trust in your ability to go out and get more. So don't look at rejecting images as an expression of failure, look at it as an expression of self-confidence.

Good Photoshop is not good photography

In the mid-1980s, a company called Aldus released a program for the Macintosh called PageMaker. This page-layout program started what was popularly known as the "desktop publishing revolution," which simply meant graphic design performed on a computer. At that time graphic design was mostly an analog process, performed on an artboard using pens, tape, glue, razor blades, and other tools. These tools required hand skills that only came from lots of practice. With desktop publishing, everyone instantly had the ability to set type, draw straight lines, create smooth curves, and so on, without having to learn any of the mechanical skills.

What this "revolution" brought about was years of really bad design.

Sure, it enabled newspapers and magazines to streamline their production workflows and to push the forefront of graphic design in new directions, but it also meant a lot of fliers on telephone poles, ads in local newspapers, and company newsletters that looked terrible. This was because people with no graphic design training suddenly decided that they could be designers for the simple fact that they had learned how to use the software. Computers were far less ubiquitous then, so someone who "knew computers" was definitely an outlier, and for a few years there were far more "desktop publishers" than there were graphic designers trained in these new tools.

Pretty much anyone can use a hammer and a screwdriver, but few of those people would suddenly decide to call themselves carpenters, so it's strange that people didn't afford the same level of respect and understanding to the profession of design. Fortunately, the designers eventually came to learn the digital options, and many amateur designers were put out of business.

Beginning photographers can suffer from the same misguided thinking when they confuse image editing skill for photographic skill. I'm not for a moment belittling good Photoshop chops. However, knowing how to use the tools to correct a photograph doesn't mean you have any idea of what a good photo is, just as knowing how to use page layout software doesn't mean you know what a well-designed page is.

We've all heard the phrase "I'll fix it in post" and certainly, digital editing tools allow you to perform fixes that would have been impossible in an earlier age. But having the ability to make technically proficient image edits isn't the same as being a good photographer. Think of it this way: it's great that an engineer can figure out how to retrofit a building to make it safer, but wouldn't you rather have a safe building to begin with?

You need good post-production skill, so keep developing those abilities, but don't think they're a substitute for knowing how to compose an image, or for understanding exposure, or for having the skill and practice of seeing in the way that a good photographer sees. Image editing skills might let you hide your photographic deficiencies for a while, but eventually, those deficiencies will catch up to you.

The most powerful tool in your image editor

While Photoshop is packed with a lot of amazing tools— content-aware fill really does seem magical—I'm constantly reminded that, possibly, the most powerful tool in anyone's image-editing arsenal is the simple Crop tool. However, in workshops and classes I'm also often reminded that people don't always think about cropping as a way to re-compose an image that has gone wrong. I think the reason has to do with what people think the Crop tool does.

If your idea of the Crop tool is that it allows you to cut the edges off of your photo, then you might be less inclined to recognize a crop as the solution to a problem in an image. But if your understanding of the Crop tool is that it lets you change the spatial relationship of things within your photo, that understanding will likely lead you to consider cropping more often.

This is exactly what the Crop tool does. When you crop the edge of a photo, elements in a scene move closer to that edge and that change in placement within the frame creates a new composition. In addition, by eliminating whatever was in the cropped area you possibly change the way the viewer's eye moves around the frame, and controlling the viewer's eye is the point of composition.

Sometimes, the effects of a crop can be shocking. Elements that seemed to have no compositional weight might be brought to the fore, or at least made more relevant. The sense of space in the scene might change. If you've radically altered the aspect ratio then you might find that you read the image in an entirely different way.

To learn to effectively use the Crop tool you might need to change the language you're using in your head while you're editing. If an image seems to have something wrong, ask yourself if it would be better if you had composed it differently. If the answer to that question is yes, then grab the Crop tool.

In praise of the small print

When famed street photographer Garry Winogrand died in 1984, he left behind more than 2,500 rolls of undeveloped, and largely uncategorized, film — roughly 100,000 frames. This was film, mind you, so even when the film was processed there was no easy way to determine the time and date of the exposures or the locations.

As digital photographers we can take some solace in the fact that our images automatically have a certain amount of useful metadata, but does that mean that our photo archive will live on in any useful way after we're gone? Right now, my photo catalog has approximately 85,000 images. Do I really expect someone else to prowl through that, trying to decode my particular system of ratings, labels and keywords? And what about the images that are on my phone? Or ones that are stored outside of the catalog, on a backup server, or in a haphazard system of digital folders?

And let's face it, the first thought when someone you know dies is not "uh oh, I'd better go get their digital photo archive in order." If years pass before that chore gets addressed then all sorts of new problems might arise, related to out-of-date software or file formats, or even an inability to plug a particular storage device into a computer. And even if, years later, someone did get access to my archive, they would find that I tend to work a particular scene a lot, so most of the images in that collection of 85,000 are non-keepers — there's a lot more rough than there are diamonds. To put it simply, sorting through someone else's photo archive would be a tedious chore.

In the old days, people kept their photos as prints, in shoe boxes or albums. Sorting through a collection of photos was something you could do as a family or group of friends, as you gathered around the images and worked together to figure out who's who and where's where. What's more, this was not necessarily something you only did as a postmortem activity. At family gatherings or holidays, pulling out the photos and comparing notes on what different people remembered about a particular event was a way to add more depth to the images — a form of metadata, in a sense.

Small photographic prints — 3x5, 4x6, 8x10 — have a power that goes beyond just the images they contain. They're artifacts. Maybe they have some deceased relative's handwriting on them, or a crease or stain caused by a memorable event. The simple act of handling them provides a sense of physically engaging with the memories that their images trigger.

Small prints are not just useful for family photos. I regularly make small prints of my fine art photos. I leave them in a big heap on a table and they sit there for years. From time to time I'll sift through them and pull some out. In print form I can easily rearrange them, or even extract one, move it to my desk, and live with it for a while. I'm surprised at how I'll often find previously unrecognized relationships between images. Or maybe I'll find that a particular sequence of images tells a good story.

A photo isn't finished until it's on paper, but it doesn't have to be on a big piece of paper in a mat and hung on a wall. Keeping prints small and tangible can give you a very different reaction to your work, one which can help you see things you haven't seen before. If printing is normally more of a "precious" process for you, then I encourage you to knock out a bunch of 4x6-inch prints and then simply live with them for a while. You might be surprised at what they teach you about your own work.

Another use for printing

A few years ago I taught a workshop alongside photojournalist Paul Taggart. We had the students working through a number of different simultaneous assignments. A few of these were photo essay assignments, so the students had a lot of different images that they needed to keep track of and, more importantly, they needed to find sequences of these images that told different stories.

Paul was adamant that they perform this sequencing on paper rather than on the computer. "If we let them sequence on the computer, they'll get distracted," he said. "They'll start worrying about how the image looks, and they'll want to correct it, rather than worrying about what's in the image, and how it fits with other images."

We gave each student a nine-foot by five-foot piece of styrofoam, which we had painted gray. For the next two weeks, each student covered their board with small prints, which they could then move about, arrange into groups, stack, spread — whatever it took to help them find the organization and sequence that they wanted. The students had to pitch their sequencing ideas to us, and one of the most frequent comments that we faced were students apologizing because the exposure was off, the color was wrong or, in one way or another, the image was not finished in the way they envisioned.

Paul had an interesting answer to that.

"Making an image look good isn't hard, and we're all photographers so we can tell from looking at a raw image whether it can be made to look good or not, so stop worrying about that. What's hard is finding a sequence of images that can tell a good story."

Even if you're working on your own, this is still good advice. Most of the time you can quickly assess whether an image can be corrected into something presentable — you don't always have to go through the process of correction to know that. Because the quality of the image is not relevant to the process, sequencing is something you can do quickly and easily and, possibly, just about anywhere.

"When I'm on the road, working on a story," Paul explained, "and I get back to the hotel at night, I'll quickly try to identify the images that I think have promise. I'll put those on a flash drive, take them down to the business center in the hotel, and print them out on their black-and-white laser printer. I've then got a stack of prints I can take back to my room and start working with on the floor or bed, or by taping them to the wall."

A side benefit of this approach is that, by delaying your post-production edits until after you've already sequenced your images, you won't waste time correcting photos that ultimately don't get used.

As you progress as a photographer, you're likely going to find yourself drawn more toward producing bodies of work rather than single, attractive images. Whether it's for an exhibition, a portfolio, or just to hang on your own walls, sequencing will be an important part of this process. Don't limit yourself to sequencing in digital form. Working with prints can be an easier, more effective way of solving the problem of how images go together.

PRESENTATION

A painter friend in Manhattan needed to visit a potential buyer. We were spending the day together so we decided that we would go to the Upper East Side, where this buyer lived, and I would sit in Central Park while my friend went to talk to this possible patron. As we walked alongside the park in what was plainly a very well-to-do neighborhood, my friend suddenly stopped.

"Oh no, I forgot to change clothes," he said.

"You look fine."

"No, I should have changed into my painter's pants and shoes."

And with that he reached down and began to rip the bottom of his nice sport shirt. Seeing my shocked expression, he explained.

"A buyer like this, they want me to be from another place, a world they don't normally interact with. A world of artists who are so into what they do that they forget to change clothes. That's part of what they're paying for when they buy a painting — a sign that they've touched that world."

In other words, he had to worry about looking like someone who didn't worry about what they look like. Presentation, it seems, really is everything.

Even if you have no desire to exhibit or sell your photos, the processes involved in creating a presentation are still a critical part of your practice. Through the curation process and the building of a portfolio to titling and artist's statements, you have a chance to critically evaluate your work and to see what exactly it is that you're presenting. During these steps you get a chance to check in with your practice routine, and to see if you're heading in the photographic direction that you want to go.

But don't worry, for the topics presented in this chapter, it doesn't matter what you wear.

Build your portfolio

My overall goal with this book is to help you understand that practice is not only necessary, it's active. You have to actively observe your practice process, figure out what works for you and change it as you grow and your skill level increases. But to know when you need to make a change, you need to know what kind of progress you've made, and to judge progress, you have to know where you've been. This is what a portfolio is for.

Most of us think of a portfolio as something that you show to someone else, when you're trying to get a gig, for example. But the most common audience for your portfolio will be yourself because, as with any practice regimen, part of your photography practice should be to regularly take stock of your work and your ability.

> If the word "portfolio" is intimidating to you, or you feel that it means, specifically, a collection of images that you show to a potential client or patron, then feel free to substitute the word "album" everywhere I'm saying "portfolio." And, although I firmly believe that you should print your portfolio, it can reside as an album in your photo organizer, a PDF, or even as a slide presentation.

At the simplest level, a portfolio is a small collection—20 to 25 images at most—that represents what you believe to be your best work. When you tell someone you're a photographer and they reply, "I would love to see some of your work," what would you show them? That's the simple criteria that you can use to build a portfolio.

The process will most likely be anything but simple. Remember, the images you choose are what you consider to be your best photos. When someone thinks about you as a photographer, these are the images that you want them to recall. These are the images that represent your photographic vision. Photos that are "close" or "good enough" or "great except for this one thing" shouldn't make the cut. If you've never done this kind of culling before, know that it can take time and might involve some (possibly unfair) self-criticism and a bit of emotional pain.

When it's done you should feel good; having 20 strong images in a portfolio is an achievement. You might also find yourself surprised. Maybe there were more good images in your library than you were expecting. Maybe there were fewer. Maybe there were ideas that you'd forgotten about that you'd like to return to or develop further. Maybe you noticed habits or themes that you'd like to continue, or others you'd like to reduce or eliminate. The best surprises are when you find great images that you previously hadn't noticed — that's not an uncommon occurrence. All of these are reasons to engage in this exercise — any one of these surprises will lead you in a new direction of practice.

As for what to do with your portfolio, that's up to you. Personally, I would print them, but, whether you do or not, you can certainly assemble an online presentation somewhere. This will take you through the process of sequencing your images, which is a valuable exercise in and of itself.

The real value of building this kind of portfolio comes later, when you do it again. That's right, you're not finished with this! In fact, you never will be. Because for this evaluation process to be useful it needs to be ongoing. As for when you should reevaluate, that's up to you. You could decide to do it once a year, on New Year's Day, perhaps, or maybe when the seasons change, or maybe every time you finish a big photo expedition or assignment. Whatever you choose, it's a good idea to have a regular rhythm to your portfolio practice.

The most important thing to understand about this re-evaluation is that you're not expanding your portfolio — you should still keep it to approximately two dozen images. What you're trying to assess is if your portfolio is still your best work. This is how your portfolio helps you track whether you're progressing. If you don't find yourself replacing images, then it's possible you're stuck and need to look at how to change your practice game to help you get back onto a path of growth. This process will also help you see how your taste is changing. For example, you might find that you don't prefer images that are as heavily edited as you used to, and so will choose to reject some images. Portfolio updating is a very simple way to evaluate your own progress.

As an alternative, you can build separate types of portfolios — landscape, portrait, whatever — and update them regularly to track progress in a particular area. Maybe you want to separate your black-and-white and color work into separate portfolios. Whatever you want to track, this is an easy way to do it.

And finally, don't worry, your portfolio doesn't mean you only have 20 great images. It means that those are just the absolute best.

Tips for building a portfolio

A portfolio is a curated selection of images that expresses something about your work. Maybe it's about who you are as a photographer, maybe it's about a particular subject. Whatever the case, here are some guidelines for assembling an effective portfolio.

Grab the viewer. Don't feel that you need to start small and build. Put a strong image right up front to grab the viewer. Give them confidence in your work. People bring their own attitude to the viewing of a photo; if you can put them in a confident mood from the start, they'll approach the rest of your work with more generosity than if you start weak.

Vary your effects. Be careful about putting images with similar properties side-by-side. For example, if you shoot a lot with a very wide-angle lens, don't sequence a bunch of those images together. The viewer will begin to question whether you can shoot well with anything but wide angles. This is true for any sort of effect — be careful of putting a bunch of heavily vignetted images together, for example.

Great photos aren't enough. Your portfolio should make the viewer want to see the next image. If you're submitting to a competitive environment, simply assembling a mess of great photos won't be enough because there will be no shortage of great photos in front of the reviewers. You need to employ additional methods to get people to turn the page.

You might know someone who's a "great storyteller." If you were to take apart how they tell a story what you would probably find is that their stories have a strong sense of rhythm. There will be emotional beats in the events they describe and tell. Story points will build in intensity until there's some kind of payoff, and then will lessen in intensity. Or, at the least, there will be a repetition of words or ideas that suddenly stops and then changes into something else.

It's easy to create rhythm in a portfolio. Group images with similar content, group images with similar compositional ideas, switch from color to black and white, and so on. The point of rhythm is two-fold. First, it's impossible to stay at a particular level of intensity without getting bored. Rhythm keeps people interested by alternating them between more and less intensity. And two, the hallmark of rhythm is repetition. If you can catch the viewer in a repeating rhythm they'll keep turning pages just to keep that rhythm going.

Know your audience. At the simplest level this means don't submit portraits to a landscape contest. The more you know about the person or institution who will be reviewing your portfolio, the better. For example, maybe a particular gallery prefers works shot in the region, maybe a particular school has a history of producing great black and white photographers. Or maybe there isn't anything you can know about your audience. Whatever the case, it's a good idea to do a little investigating.

Less is more. If there's a limit to the number of images that you can include, then obviously you have to follow that limit (see the next point). If there's not a limit, then err on the side of fewer images. Far fewer images. A well-crafted portfolio of 18-25 images will always be stronger than a portfolio of 36 images. There's nothing wrong with leaving the viewer wanting more.

Follow the instructions. If you're building a portfolio to send to some sort of adjudicated event—a school or contest, for example—then be certain that you've followed every instruction to the letter. When you're a judge sitting in front of a stack of 200 portfolios, your first pass will not be to find great work, it will be to find any reason to eliminate someone. Finding someone who didn't follow the instructions is the easiest way to do this.

Change it up. If you have a portfolio that's visible to the public—a place where you send potential clients, say—then don't leave it alone. People who come back to look at it again will want to see change. Shuffle new material through your portfolio, try different rhythms and arrangements. Most importantly, recognize that changing your portfolio is a chance to be critical and grow. Work that you thought was great five years ago might look less sophisticated to you now. That's not bad news! It's a sign that you've changed and possibly improved.

As with everything I say, these are not steadfast rules. These are not the only concerns when making a portfolio, and there will be exceptions to everything I've presented here. However, these are safe guidelines for getting started. Of course, a simple way to get better at portfolio-building is to look at a lot of portfolios to see what you think works and what doesn't.

Organically building and maintaining a portfolio can be daunting, but it's something you should engage in regularly, not because you'll necessarily show it to other people, but because it gives you a chance to self-evaluate. In addition to giving you a chance to feel good about your work, the process will help you find areas of focus for your future practice and growth.

A strong body of work takes time

Here's a weird thing about photography: when you have less experience, it's easier to take a great photo. Or rather, it's easier to take what you think is a great photo.

Over years of teaching, I've noticed that most photographers go through very specific stages during their first few years of shooting. There's the stage where they recognize how compelling textures can be, there's the stage where they recognize strong lines, the stage where they advance that recognition to shapes, the stage where they begin to see the power of dark shadows. Similar stages of recognition continue throughout your photographic life, but the bulk of them come at the beginning.

These are necessary evolutionary steps and they can lead to enjoyable, capable, well-executed photos. To a more experienced eye, these images often look like "student work." I'm not saying that photographers at this level of experience aren't capable of taking fresh, exciting photos. But much of what they shoot will be explorations of a visual sense that is still new and developing.

You can see these same stages in the portfolios of some of the great early photographers. Alfred Stieglitz, Paul Strand, the Westons — they all went through these same stages. However, at the time, such photos were new to everyone, and so they seemed like new visions. Now it's easier to recognize some of their photos as student work.

Having your visual sense activated like this is fun and exciting. And in the early stages you can make progress quickly. You might feel like every week you're seeing more and more, and it all feels new and fresh. And because all this is new to you, the images that you shoot will be very exciting to you.

When things are feeling this exciting, it's easy to take the jump to "This is going great — I'm gonna start trying to sell stuff!" Under the best of circumstances, the commercial photography world can be brutal, while the fine art world can be downright cruel. When you're in the early stages of learning, you don't need to be exposed to the fickle, somewhat arbitrary verdict of commerce-driven aesthetics. At the same time, you don't necessarily want to enter into a safe, comfortable exhibit situation, either. You need intelligent, learned criticism when you start out. Sales at a local community art fair might be a great confidence booster, but they might also encourage habits and aesthetics that will keep you from growing, at a time when you really need to be learning what makes a great photograph.

It can take years of study and practice before you have a solid portfolio for either commercial or fine art work. Don't rush it. In fact, enjoy the fact that you don't need to worry about it. This time when your eyes are opening up and seeing things for the first time is yours. Enjoy it. As you get more experienced, it can often be harder to feel the kind of simple joy that you can have when you're starting out.

Maybe you don't know enough yet

One of the most famous photographs ever taken is an Ansel Adams image called *Moonrise, Hernandez*. The sun was setting very quickly and Adams knew he only had enough time to get one exposure of the scene. He was working with a large format camera, and he said because of the nature of his exposure, this photo was very difficult to print.

What's interesting is that he returned to this image and kept printing it again and again throughout his life. With *Moonrise, Hernandez*, you'll be able to tell when in Adams' life he made the print you're seeing because as he got older, and printed it again, he always printed the sky darker. He didn't do that because he thought the earlier ones were wrong. He did that because his aesthetic had changed, and his understanding of tonal relationships and the power of tonal relationships altered, as he got older.

> If you ever get a chance to see a print of this in a gallery or a museum, do it. Real prints generally look quite different from reproductions, and are often closer to the photographer's intent.

I have a few images that I've been editing for years. I don't get up and work on them every day; I've just never gotten them quite right. Every once in a while I return to them to see if I can figure out how to make them work. I've made some improvements, but I still don't feel confident that I've "solved" these images in the best way. It's entirely possible, of course, that these images are simply unsuccessful; there are plenty of times when I edit a photo and realize the image isn't going to work, no matter what I do. With these images I'm referring to, I feel different. I have a sense that there is a solution to them, but I just don't know enough yet to find it. And so I set the images aside, and return to them from time to time. It might take years, but my hope is that eventually something will change. Maybe I'll learn something, or my perspective will change, or my aesthetic will change so that I can go back to these images and know what I need to do.

We live in an era where we shove images onto social media and then move along to the next image. There's power in that, but it's also important to take time with your images. Sometimes that might mean years, and sometimes that time might involve not editing them, while you wait for necessary growth so that you can understand what an image needs.

Wrestling with the artist's statement

I don't know you, of course, or where you are or what you might be thinking, but I feel fairly confident in making a prediction about you: you hate the idea of having to write a statement or explanation about your photographs. I know this because everyone hates writing those statements. The good news is that you aren't facing an obstacle that doesn't hound every photographer who decides to exhibit their work. We all have to do it, and most of us hate it.

In the essays on portfolios, I talked about how assembling a portfolio is a chance to evaluate your own work, so as to adjust your practice to shore up any weaknesses you might be experiencing. Writing an artist's statement is a similar process, but it is one that hits some different areas. And so I would argue that, if you have assembled a particular body of work — maybe you've been working on a project around a particular subject matter, or you've noticed that you have some images that fit well together compositionally or thematically — then you should try writing an artist's statement, even if you don't have a need for one right now.

"I'm a photographer, not a writer, and my photos should stand on their own," is the most common pushback against the artist's statement. Writing a statement does not make you less of a photographer, or take the place of any of your images. Rather, it forces you to think about your work in a critical way, and more importantly, demands that you figure out if you like the work, and why. If you can't explain why you like the work, why should you expect anyone else to be able to explain why they like it?

Whether you like the work or not, there is a reason that you have chosen to group specific images together and you need to know what that reason is. Even if you don't want to explain it to someone else, knowing will help you ensure that your reasoning is sound and that your images back up your idea. If writing the statement feels redundant and only convinces you that you were right to group those images together, that's great — you can feel more confident about the work. But writing a statement might lead you to conclude that some images don't belong, or that you need some additional images, or that your sequencing is wrong. In the process of writing the statement, you might flesh out your idea in a way that leads you to other ideas, and new, future photo projects.

Most importantly, writing a statement forces you to express, in plain language, why you like the work and what you might be trying to say or reveal with it. If you've never made such an explicit statement about the work then you might be surprised to find that the statement isn't clear enough, or that you don't actually agree with the statement or, on very rare occasions, that you don't actually like the work. Those are all very valuable pieces of information.

You don't have to like writing an artist's statement, but you do have to do it if you're going to present a body of work to other people.

Titles

Whether or not you like titles on photos, it is the current fashion, so if you're going to exhibit or sell your images somewhere, you'll likely be expected to provide titles with them.

Titling is a tricky endeavor. On the one hand, a title can give the viewer context — a specific understanding of time or place. Your title might give the viewer some idea of your artistic intent. On the other hand, having a title might constrain the viewer. A title that's very specific might make it harder for them to have their own honest interpretation, reaction and feeling about an image.

The best way to learn about how to title your images is to pay attention to your reaction to the titles of other people's photos. Personally, for photojournalism or other documentary projects, I find that I like titles, as long as they're titles that answer the simple questions that I have. "Where was this shot?" "Who is this?" "When was this?" In documentary images, those specifics are often important to the viewer's satisfaction.

With fine art images I often have very practical questions that nag at me, even when the image is not meant to be a straight documentary work. If you show me a beautiful image of a spectacular building or landscape, I can't help but want to know where that is. With portraits, I like to know the subject's name, though I'm not sure why. I think it feels like an introduction, and that's comforting to me.

For very formal work — abstract work of pure photographic form — I ignore the title. In those instances, I don't want to know what the photographer was thinking or feeling or intending. I want to have my own reaction and I don't want them to mess it up for me.

Again, those are my reasons and they are in no way correct or gospel. I present them here as examples of the kinds of ways that you might react to a title. If you spend some time looking at titles across several genres of photography, you'll probably quickly figure out if you like poetic, descriptive titles, or titles that are more practical. Regardless, you should think about titles.

What does a sale mean?

As I write this, we're about six months into the COVID-19 outbreak of 2020. With the outbreak, I've been delighted to see that many people quickly came to understand that isolation and social distancing didn't have to mean a cessation of their photography. There's been a lot of great, responsibly shot imagery showing up on social media feeds. That said, much has changed for photographers, with one of the biggest questions being "what will become of photo galleries?"

Personally, I have no idea, but I've been thinking about something my friend Sonja Schenk told me a few months ago. Sonja is an accomplished painter and she pointed out that, historically, much of the best painting work — and a significant amount of breakthroughs in the art — have come during times when painters couldn't sell their work for one reason or another. Whether it was due to plague, war, economic collapse or political turmoil, when painters have realized that the market for their work was off-limits, they have often used those opportunities to experiment, or work on personal ideas that they'd been putting off because they were committed to more commercial work.

In other words, in normal times painters often paint what sells, not what they're interested in. That, of course, is true for all disciplines, and the question of "selling out" is one that artists have struggled with for as long as there's been money.

I am not arguing that sales are bad. However, I do think it's important to pay attention to how selling your work can affect your practice and development as a photographer. Following the market will not necessarily lead you to grow as a photographer, or to achieve the skill set and vision that you might want. (Obviously, if your goal is some form of commercial photography, then sales are the most important benchmark. For this essay I'm talking about those who have a goal of fine art photography.)

Whether you sell your work or not, you should be photographing for yourself, not for other people. You should be working to satisfy your own creative goals and to achieve images that match your own aesthetic. As a practicing photographer, you have spent many hours studying photos and photographic technique and have trained your eye to better see both the world and other photographs. In other words, as a photographer, you probably have a more developed aesthetic than the average consumer of photography. Following sales, then, may not be the path that leads you to photographs that satisfy your own aesthetic. While sales can be exciting, straying for too long from that personal path can lead to disappointment and frustration.

Perhaps the most important thing to understand about sales is that they are a reward, and therefore reinforcement, for certain photographic behaviors. There's nothing wrong with selling, and there's nothing wrong with trying to shoot images that sell. But be aware that photographic practices that lead to prints that sell may be separate from the photographic practices that lead you to images that resonate with you, and satisfy your own personal goals.

Getting your project out into the world

One of life's difficult lessons is that doing good work is not always enough; many times the world doesn't notice. Photographer Steve Simon does really good work. He also understands the importance of hustle and has possibly the best hustle story I've ever heard:

"I had just moved to New York City, as a freelance photographer, when 9/11 happened. Like the rest of the city, I was in shock, but as a photographer, I wandered with my cameras. I happened upon the Ground Zero area. I was kind of avoiding it, but when I was around that area, I noticed the reactions of people, and it was very intense, and I thought to myself, well maybe I can do a project where I could document what had happened through the faces of the people who felt compelled to come and see it for themselves. So from the end of September to the end of December I shot with my Nikon F100 and Tri-X film. I shot 100 rolls.

"I had all this material, I love books, and I thought 'this could be an interesting, important book.' So I put together a book dummy. I took what I thought were the strongest pictures, and put together this black and white book dummy, and I called it *Empty Sky*, and I sent it out to all the publishers that do photo books.

"And then I started getting the rejection letters. Some of the rejection letters were nice, some of them gave me some advice, and I would try and make it better, if that was possible. I wasn't going to give up. So I continued to try and get this thing published, and with all these rejections coming in, I thought I would try something different.

"In the building where I live, above where I am, Susan Sontag lived in one of the penthouses. She has a connection to photography that I think most students of photography would be familiar with — she wrote a book called *On Photography*, which is kind of required reading in most photo programs. So I thought, 'if I can get Susan Sontag to write a forward for my book, that might help push me over the edge to get this thing published.'

"So I brought my book dummy to my doorman and asked if he could get it to Susan Sontag, and he said sure. And he did! I know this because the next day, the very next day, I got a call from Susan Sontag's assistant. He said, 'She probably won't have time to even look at it for a few weeks, maybe I should save you some time and just send it back.' I told him that I had no expectations, I just wanted her to see it, and I asked if there was any way he could show it to her. At the end of the conversation I felt confident he was going to.

"So I continued. I continued trying to get it published. I continued to get rejection letters. And then out of the blue I got a call from this guy. He said, 'Hey my name's Andy Levin, I'm a photographer in New York City. I just bought a copy of your book dummy from a guy selling it on Seventh Avenue for four dollars.'

"Of course I was thinking 'What?' I mean, I was secretly happy he paid four dollars for it, but I was still completely confused. Andy went on to say, 'Yeah, the guy that sold it to me said he got it from Susan Sontag's garbage.'

"I was trying to process all this and figure out what was going on, and all while Andy was saying 'I have this friend at *Life* magazine. She's publishing this commemorative edition, can I show it to her?' Obviously I said yeah, please do.

"And that's how I ended up getting eight pages in this *Life* publication, *The American Spirit*. I got my biggest paycheck since arriving in New York City. And, with the credibility of being in that publication, I was able to find a small publisher in my native Montreal to publish a bilingual edition of *Empty Sky*. And it all came from Susan Sontag's garbage. I know this because I went back to Ralph, the door guy, and I said, 'Ralph, you're not going to believe this; this guy said he bought my book at Seventh out of Susan Sontag's garbage.' And Ralph said 'Oh yeah, that's Steve.'

"It turns out that Steve is a guy in the building who sorts through the recycling to find things to sell on Craigslist or on the sidewalk. So it just re-affirmed for me that you can't give up. Keep putting the work out there. Put it out everywhere. There's no bad publicity and there are no bad recycling bins."

CODA

"There are many teachers who could ruin you. Before you know it, you could be a pale copy of this teacher or that teacher. You have to evolve on your own."

— Berenice Abbott

Developing a practice strategy

There are two major things that I hope you take away from this book. The first is the understanding that regular practice is necessary if you want to improve as a photographer, and the second is that figuring out how to practice is, itself, a creative act. To practice effectively you have to analyze your weaknesses, concoct a plan to address those weaknesses and then figure out how to implement that plan in a way that will keep you engaged and motivated. What's more you'll have to repeat this process, for a practice plan is not static. It needs to change as your skill level changes.

Here are some suggestions for developing a practice strategy. Like everything else in this book, you need to decide whether the suggestions here work for you, or if they need to be modified or skipped altogether.

What do you need to practice?

Your first step in building a practice strategy is to figure out what you need to practice. The simple answer? You need to practice the things you're not good at. You might have some weak spots that are obvious to you — perhaps you don't feel confident about your compositions — but it can often be difficult to identify a particular area that you feel you need to work on.

It might be easier to assess your weaknesses if you break down the process of photography into three categories: technical, aesthetic/creative and somatic. Technical covers all of the mechanical things you must know to take a picture: exposure theory, camera handling, post-production tasks, printing, and more. Aesthetic/creative are the non-technical decisions: framing, depth of field, use of light and shadow, use of color and tonality and so on. Somatic issues are the things you can practice to improve your ability to recognize subject matter and to see clearly.

What follows are some possibilities from each category. If you can think of others you should definitely add them to the lists. You can pick one thing to practice intently or you can mix it up. I find that the technical things are the easiest to practice, so working one or two of those alongside creative and somatic topics can help keep you motivated and engaged.

Technical

- **Shooting in focus.** This can cover everything from understanding your camera's autofocus system to understanding how to prevent blur caused by camera shake to knowing how to get the depth of field that you want.

- **Shooting moving subjects.** Focusing on something that is moving toward you is tricky, as is panning to follow a subject moving past you. Both of these require practice and an understanding of how much blur is caused by a given shutter speed.
- **Low-light shooting.** Balancing shutter speed, camera shake, and motion blur against the noise caused by higher ISOs requires experimentation and varies from camera to camera. What's more, you've got to be able to implement the appropriate strategy quickly, if you're shooting in an environment where things are changing rapidly.
- **Intentional underexposure.** Crushing shadows can be a very useful tool in building compositions. Learning to recognize when a shadow in the real world can be made more useful through intentional darkening is a good thing to practice.
- **Intentional overexposure.** When should you blow out highlights? Practicing doing that will help you develop an aesthetic for when highlights can be overrun as well as the technical skill for achieving the look you want.
- **Understanding the histogram.** Whether it's an in-camera histogram or the one in your image editor, practicing histogram analysis is an essential step in improving as a photographer.
- **Printing.** This is a big subject, as there are many steps involved in printing, but making lots of prints is the only way to improve.
- **Controlling geometry through camera position and focal length.** You can radically change the sense of organization and depth in a scene depending on where you stand and what focal length you use. Experimenting with such choices isn't always something you have the freedom to do while shooting, so practicing with these decisions is a real luxury.
- **Lighting.** Whether it's natural light, strobes, or continuous light, taking the time to slowly consider the changes that occur when you modify, move, and control light is incredibly valuable. This is another one of those things that you don't always have the freedom to experiment with in the "real world" so contriving situations to explore during practice is essential for improving your lighting skills.
- **Specialized shooting.** Macro, astro, underwater, portrait, sports, wildlife, aerial — different photographic specialties each have their

own specific technical challenges and difficulties. Start adding those to this list and you should have plenty of things to practice.
- **Specialized post-production.** If you are interested in photos that have special post-production needs—facial retouching, focus stacking, stitching, compositing, and so on—you've got lots to work on.
- **Access.** It might seem strange to list this as a technical skill, but it's definitely a practical skill that is essential, especially if you're interested in photojournalism or photo essays. Very often the key to those great images you see in magazines is not camera skill but skill at getting access. Choose something you don't see every day — lions (outside of cages), submarines, rodeo clowns — and figure out how you might get access to such things.
- **Special camera features.** Perhaps your camera has built-in focus stacking, or geotagging, or film simulations or white balance bracketing. You don't want to learn these features at the moment that you need them. Practicing with them is also a great way to determine if these are features that are really worth learning.
- **Quality of your edits.** It's possible to edit too much, to push edits too far. Experimenting with different levels of specific edits is good practice. How much is too much sharpening? Are you learning to notice when you've lost detail because you've pushed a color change too far? Don't be surprised if, over time, you start to find that a super-saturated image doesn't look as good as it once did.

Aesthetic/Creative

The obvious catch-all item here would be "composition." We all probably wonder, with any given photo, if there was a better composition to be had. Rather than simply list composition as something to practice, I'm going to list some particular compositional ideas.

- **Center of the frame.** It's easy to think of this as "simple" composition, but framing things in the dead center of the frame can be very powerful. When does it work and when does it not? Just as importantly, when can you leave the center of the frame completely empty? That leads to...
- **Composing on the edges.** What kind of compositions can you make by placing subject matter on the sides, and what else do you need to make a balanced image? (Note that I'm not talking about "thirds" composing, but placing things on the very edge.)

- **Aspect ratio.** Choice of aspect ratio is one of the most important decisions that you will make. Experiment with several, on the same subject matter, to see how you have to mix things up with different aspect ratios to get a good photo.
- **Cropping.** This is a good exercise for those days when you can't go shooting. Work through your library and experiment with different crops. This is a great way to learn when a crop can save a photo. Doing this a lot will change the way you compose in the field.
- **Layering.** I'm not talking about Photoshop layers, but rather the idea of relating objects to each other when they sit on different planes. This is pretty easy to do while looking through the viewfinder, but it takes a lot of practice to be able to recognize potential layered relationships with the naked eye. Renting or borrowing an extremely long lens is a great way to practice this.
- **Exposure choices and composition.** How does your composition change as you create new compositional elements through exposure? Dark shadows, bright highlights, low-contrast — all of these things impact composition, and intentionally practicing with these ideas is invaluable.
- **Color or black and white.** Practice seeking out black and white subject matter or, conversely, subject matter that requires color. Back at home, practice your black and white conversion skills or your color enhancement.
- **Less is more.** What is the bare minimum that you can have in the frame and still have a working photo of a subject? Your creative skills will improve tremendously as you learn what's actually necessary to make a photo.
- **Specialized composition.** As with technical skills, different genres of photography have specific compositional needs that require practice.
- **Photo books and galleries.** I would hope I wouldn't have to still say this, but I'm going to anyway. Looking at and studying photos is the best way to develop an aesthetic and an understanding of what makes a great image.

Somatic

- **Presence.** Any activity you can engage in that increases your sense of immediate awareness and presence, and calms the chatter in your head, will help your ability to see. Meditation, yoga, being attacked by a wild animal. Anything is fair game if it works.
- **Another visual art.** Drawing, painting, sculpting — these require you to look at the world with a level of detail that you don't always employ as a photographer. You'll see the world differently after doing any of these activities.
- **Photo books.** I'm not trying to be annoying by including this again. Look at enough photos and you will begin to see differently.

Making a plan

Once you know what you want to practice you need to find a way to practice it. Internet searches will often lead to good exercises for specific issues. You can download my free exercise book (cdp.pub/exercisebook) and you can keep an eye on my Practicing Photographer video series — if you're a LinkedIn Learning subscriber — where I often issue challenges to perform specific exercises. (If you're not a subscriber, the current week's episode is always free at cdp.pub/linkedin.)

It's also possible to create your own exercises, and one of the easiest ways is to think about extremes. If you don't feel comfortable with the execution or application of different depths of field then practice shooting exclusively with either extremely deep or extremely shallow depth of field. Limit yourself to a specific focal length to explore particular geometric or layering possibilities at that length. And so on.

Anything that makes you see differently can yield a good somatic exercise — overexpose every shot by 2 stops; spend a day shooting at extremely shallow depth of field. These types of exercises will often open your eyes to new subject matter and new compositional ideas.

Once you've got some exercises that you think are appropriate you can make some decisions about how much and how often you want to practice. Those are very personal decisions but I recommend sticking to whatever you decide for a specific amount of time. A big part of getting better at practice is proving to yourself that you can and will do it.

If you want, you can try to set a goal, but depending on what it is you're practicing, a goal can be hard to quantify. And, as I've already mentioned, your goal should be to practice.

Evaluation

At some point you need to see if you're getting better at the things you're practicing. Give yourself some time to practice and then, after you've got some work to look at, sit down and evaluate it. It doesn't matter how often you do this, but it is an important step to take.

A few last pointers:

You need to devise a practice scheme that works to your advantage. If you're the type of person who needs to conquer extremely difficult goals, then set an aggressive practice plan. If you prefer to have a practice regimen that doesn't feel adversarial, then craft a strategy that will let you feel some success without wearing you out.

If you start practicing and aren't enjoying it, then set it aside. Don't set it aside for too long, because you don't want to break momentum, but practice is only beneficial if you're open to it.

Finally, be creative. Be creative in your assessment of your problems, in your ideas about how to tackle those problems and in the ways you keep yourself motivated and engaged. This is your practice — your creation — make it your own.

Is my practice successful?

We've discussed two different skill sets, the skill of photography, and the skill of practicing photography. Hopefully, you've come to an understanding that practice requires a great deal of thought, consideration, and experimentation. Maybe not as much as that which you're actually practicing, but enough that it can support a book-length discussion. We have covered ideas for evaluating whether your photography is improving, but how do you evaluate the effectiveness of your practice regimen?

Obviously, if your photos are improving, then your practice methodology must be working pretty well. But a practice regimen should do more than simply make you a better photographer. It should keep you engaged and interested, it should help you to grow as a person by expanding your connection to and understanding of the world around you. As I said at the beginning, your goal should not be to take great pictures, but to practice, so you want to make sure that your practice zone is a place you want to be. Practice should inspire you; it should not be a chore.

So how do you evaluate your current practice regimen? I don't know. What's more, I can't know, because what will make effective practice for you is personal. It's something you have to figure out on your own through self-reflection and experimentation. You have to try different approaches and follow what feels right to you.

The most important thing to remember is that, in trying to find a practice scheme that works for you, you have to be creative. Figuring out how to practice is an exercise in the creative process itself. There are no rights or wrongs, and sometimes you have to take radical steps. I know a bass player who said his practicing improved greatly once he made certain that there was always a bass in every room of his house. (When asked what his wife thought of this, he replied "she's not crazy about it, but the bass paid for the house, so she lets it slide.")

While I can't tell you a specific plan for practicing, here are a few more ideas to think about when experimenting with your own scheme.

- **Leave yourself wanting more.** Don't practice until you're burned out — quit practicing when things are still going well, so that you'll be eager to get back to it next time. The image of the artist wringing himself out with creative process is romantic and all, but it doesn't lead to longevity. Rest and recovery is as important in photography as it is to an athlete.

- **Manage the parts you don't like.** Maybe you're not crazy about post-production. That's fine, but be aware that you might have a tendency to put it off so that, when you are finally forced to deal with post-production, you'll have a crushing workload. If there are aspects of photography you don't enjoy, mix them in with other bits so that you don't have to wallow in them.
- **Never pass up an opportunity to learn about photography.** If you happen to meet the world's greatest photographer of, say, sports memorabilia, and they're willing to show you how they work, take that opportunity, even if you have no interest in what they're shooting. You don't know what you'll be able to take from their experience but, more importantly, you don't know what you're going to be interested in shooting later. No matter how thrilled you are about a particular type of shooting right now, there's a good chance that you're going to grow tired of it. The more you've seen of other aspects of photography, the easier it will be for you to find something new to be interested in.
- **Never pass up an opportunity to learn about anything else.** If photography is a way of expressing something about who you are, then the more you grow as a person, the more you'll have to say and explore with your camera. In other words, the practice of photography may not always involve photography.
- **Never let practicing become a chore.** Think about my friend who was going to practice on his wedding day, because it relaxes him. That's what practice is supposed to be. If it's not that for you, then you need to make a change to your practice scheme. And don't rule out the idea that you may need to get away from photography for a while. If you feel burned out, then it might be time to take a break. Don't worry, if photography is something that really does matter to you, then you will be drawn back to it.

Finally, I want to encourage you to appreciate where you're at right now. Remember, there's no ending to this. There will always be more to learn and explore so don't ignore where you're at now because you're in a hurry to get down the road. That doesn't mean you can't strive to improve but really, chill out.

I'm happy to say that, while I hated practicing as a kid, I don't anymore. And not because of what it's done for my photography, but because I feel like I have a better understanding of photography as a medium. I'm more intelligent in the way that I look at images, and I like the relationship that I have with my visual sense now. Taking better photographs has been a great bonus.

Other Resources

You can find all of the links referred to in this book, as well as additional resources related to practicing, on *The Practicing Photographer* support page, here: **cdp.pub/PPsupport**

Alternatively, you can scan the QR Code below to view that page.

Ben's Practicing Photographer series on LinkedIn Learning can be found here: **cdp.pub/linkedin**

If you'd like to get in touch with us, you can send us email at:

>ben@completedigitalphotography.com
>rick@completedigitalphotography.com

www.ingramcontent.com/pod-product-compliance
Lightning Source LLC
Chambersburg PA
CBHW071601220526
45469CB00003B/1087